A Voyage by Dhow

Norman Lewis was a well-known travel writer and the author of thirteen novels as well as fifteen works of non-fiction. He died in 2003.

NORMAN LEWIS

A VOYAGE BY DHOW

AND OTHER PIECES

PICADOR

First published 2001 by Jonathan Cape Ltd

This edition published 2003 by Picador
an imprint of Pan Macmillan Ltd
Pan Macmillan, 20 New Wharf Road, London N1 9RR
Basingstoke and Oxford
Associated companies throughout the world
www.panmacmillan.com

ISBN 0 330 41209 4

1 3 5 7 9 8 6 4 2

A CIP catalogue record for this book is available from
the British Library.

Printed and bound in Great Britain by
Mackays of Chatham plc, Chatham, Kent

All Pan Macmillan titles are available from
www.panmacmillan.com
or from Bookpost by telephoning 01624 677237

To Cass, Jack and Scott –

in the hope that others will follow

CONTENTS

A VOYAGE BY DHOW

I

BACK IN MY early days my interests in photography and
foreign languages, particularly Arabic, came to the
attention of a Rex Stevens of the Colonial Office. In the
spring of 1937 he called on me to enquire whether I
might be interested in a journey to the Yemen, which
until then had been hardly visited by Western travellers,
and of which little was known.

Having succeeded in awakening my interest, Stevens
passed me on to the Foreign Office, where an official
outlined the drawbacks to a small expedition of the kind
he had in mind. Such unsolicited incursions were regarded
by the country's suspicious and xenophobic rulers as
espionage, to be punished by chopping off the offender's
head. 'So far only two Englishmen have travelled in the
country. There are no roads as we understand them.
There's no electricity and you will be unable to eat the
food. I would strongly recommend a further discussion
with Stevens before you commit yourself.'

When I saw Stevens again, he shrugged his shoulders.

'These men are professional pessimists,' he said. 'Do you still feel you might want to go ahead?' I told him I did. 'In that case you must meet Ladislas Farago,' he said. 'He'll be coming along.'

'Didn't he write that book about Abyssinia?'

'He certainly did, and if you haven't read it I've got a copy here.'

Stevens fumbled in his briefcase and brought out a copy of *Abyssinia on the Eve*, which at that moment was in all the bookshops. 'It's the most extraordinary book of its kind I've ever read. Absolutely riveting. Farago's a remarkable man. Anyway, why don't you join us?' Stevens said. 'You'd find it of immense interest, I assure you, and full of amazing adventures.'

'I can imagine,' I said.

In the end it was decided that I should meet Farago if that could be done, and later that day I took a phone call from Stevens to say that this had been arranged for the following Friday.

This gave me a couple of days to read the book, and I settled down to an account of the extraordinary year Farago had spent in Abyssinia.

Farago was a journalist who worked for the Associated Press. He was Hungarian born; a great miser and bluffer. I found him flamboyant and unreliable. A couple of years earlier he had been sent to Abyssinia on the eve of the Italian invasion. There he had discovered a country that had never freed itself from the Middle Ages – nor had it wished to do so – ruled by Haile Selassie, its emperor, and a tiny aristocracy which enjoyed total power. In Abyssinia, they had even dispensed with prisons. If a man killed another the nearest armed guard would execute him on the spot, and there were buffalo-hide whips and branding irons ready in the street to be used on minor criminals. Proven liars were scourged, and debtors chained to their creditors. Slave markets existed in the remoter towns, and Farago described naked slaves of both sexes being exhibited for sale.

On the Friday, as arranged, the meeting with Ladislas Farago took place in Stevens' office. My first impression of Farago was favourable. Reading his book I had been carried along by a robust sense of humour and now I was impressed by his modesty – highly commendable in a successful author. It was evident that he had experienced considerable relief at being able to put Abyssinia behind him at last. In his view nothing in European history had existed to compare with the tragic condition of the poor in that country.

So had he finally turned his back on the place? Stevens asked. Farago raised his eyes to the ceiling. 'I have no plans to go back,' he said.

Stevens turned to the Yemen project, which had clearly been under discussion before my arrival. 'So, Ladislas, I can take it you're quite happy with what's suggested?' he asked.

Farago laughed. 'I have to do something for a living. Who do we see about all the details?'

'No one but me, I'm afraid,' Stevens said. 'We're dealing with a closed country. There's no one we can talk to except a number of Bedouins who trade across the border. We know nothing of what goes on at the top, which is what interests us. We're starting from scratch.'

'When do you expect we'll be making a move?' I asked.

'As soon as we can. Sir Bernard Reilly, our man over

there, is giving us a letter for the King and I've managed to fix up passages on a dhow from Aden. The first thing we do when we get there is see the skipper – he'll ask us to sign a paper saying that we believe in God. Be another week or so before they collect all the passengers and we can set sail,' Stevens replied.

'Things move slowly,' I said.

'They do, but you soon get used to it,' Stevens told us. 'The only port in the Yemen is Hodeidah. It takes five to fifteen days to get there, according to the weather. What happens next, heavens only knows.'

'And once again, what is the objective of the expedition?' I asked. It was a question which produced one of Stevens' secret smiles.

'The answer,' he said, 'is that we will gain valuable information. You will busy yourself with your camera, and Ladislas, I'm sure, will write another excellent book. Just think of the photographic possibilities. It's still illegal to take photographs in the Yemen. Did you know that?' he asked.

'No, I did not.'

'Something to do with the Prophet's ban on graven images. Which being the case, you'll want to get shots of practically everything you see.'

'Naturally.'

Little remained to be settled after that. Stevens spoke to his travel agent, and a week later we boarded the SS *Llansteffan Castle*. We reached Aden in nine days.

II

Aden was then one of the great destinations of the world.

Sitting in the middle of the trade route to India, it was of immense strategic importance and had been ruled by the British since the 1830s. A constant, almost uncontrollable, influx of travellers poured through it, as if through a cosmic filter, from all parts of the Eastern and Western worlds. Newcomers passed through a climate of bewilderment, frustration, hope, relief and despair before finding salvation in the neutrality of a hotel.

Though we had arrived late in the day, the heat was still intolerable. Fortunately the Marina Hotel to which we had been delivered possessed a roof terrace on which beds were lined up ready for the night. From this point there was a distant view of what we were assured was the last of the 'Towers of Silence', with vultures flapping over it round a corpse abandoned for disposal. The mutterings and squawks of nocturnal animals destroyed any hopes of sleep and I got up and moved down to the bar, which was still open. Here I was instantly approached by a courteous young man who handed me a visiting card engraved with his name, Joseph, and his profession: Senior Officer's Pimp. We talked for a while of his occupation and he assured me that Aden City and the smaller towns of the Protectorate possessed in all 8,000 prostitutes, and that those under his protection were not only of exceptional beauty and charm but had the education necessary to be included at reasonable prices in any family party. There were a few who could perform tricks at such gatherings, even causing the guests' enemies to disappear and be seen no more, although they naturally demanded a higher fee.

Stevens was soon busy making our arrangements. After a visit to Sir Bernard Reilly, the Governor, he was handed a letter to the Imam Yahya – at the time on the verge of official recognition as the Yemeni king. Sir Bernard hoped that our visit might do something to improve the somewhat flaccid relationship between Britain and the Yemen in recent years. Obtaining our permit, however, proved difficult. Money could provide a variety of entertainment in Aden but when it came to taking a dhow to the Yemen even financial solidity came second to religious faith.

We were soon assured that, by the greatest of good fortune, a dhow had just arrived in port that would serve our purposes. It would shortly be taking cargo for destinations on the Red Sea, including Hodeidah. Unfortunately it had run into a storm on its way from Al Mukalla, necessitating repairs involving an uncertain number of weeks. We were taken to inspect it and welcomed on board. It bore the name *El Haq* (Truth), and had been somewhat nonchalantly berthed in an angle of the waterway. It smelt of bad breath, and a man in a yellow jacket of the kind in compulsory use where outbreaks of the plague were suspected was splashing the deck with disinfectant from a can, while another had withdrawn to a corner for evening prayer. The inflated corpse of a dog drifted past on a sluggish current. The dhow was smaller than expected and would have been much improved by fresh paint. It was impossible to ignore the massive, roughly carpentered chair in its surrounding cage, known in Arabic as 'the place of ease', which would be hoisted high in the air over the waves as soon as the ship was under way.

This safe area on a coast elsewhere unprotected from the weather had assured the wealth of one of the most prosperous purely maritime cities on earth. Yet making our way back to the urban centre we found ourselves on streets in which two or sometimes three buildings had been squeezed into gaps left where one had fallen. The old white houses down by the port were splashed by mud thrown up by vehicles driven at top speed, and first- and second-floor windows dribbled slops into the street. Held up in a traffic jam there was no escaping the sight of a group of children who had gathered to stone a three-legged puppy trapped in a doorway. Aden was on its way to becoming the capital of the Middle East, but outside the showpiece of its centre, burdened with wealth as it was, there was something about it that was repellent and cruel.

III

By the end of the sixth week of our stay, we had become very familiar with the situation in Aden. Investigating the city, we had, worryingly, identified many Italian soldiers in mufti, though Ladislas assured me that they had been drawn there by the presence of a singular attraction. This was, in fact, the best-kept brothel in the Mediterranean, with a complex of charming and spotless chalets said to have been designed by a lapsed Roman Catholic priest, based on a vision of Paradise that had drawn him to the place. It was heavy with the perfume of the jasmine plants that trailed over all the houses, and ruled over by a dazzling young lady of fourteen named 'Halva' (Sweetness), who made no charge for her services for suitors who presented themselves with an acceptable poem. But we had also soon become aware of the presence of many secret agents, and there was no longer any doubt in my mind, and certainly none in Farago's, as to the immediate purpose of our presence there.

This had been instantly confirmed when, on the spur of the moment, I had visited Stevens in the lodgings he had taken to escape the noise of the hotel. He had put aside a map he had been studying but it was clearly one of southern Yemen, showing an area encircled in red ink. A whisky bottle close at hand may have accounted for his immediate frankness. He shook his head. 'Really it's all a matter of who gets there first – the Italians or us,' he said. 'Everybody realizes that something has to happen. Any leads on the situation? I suppose it's early days.'

'I wasn't sure how urgent this was,' I said. 'I talked to a man who could be useful yesterday. Belongs to an organization called the Whisperers, based in Lahej. He could find us a professional guide and bodyguards if necessary.'

'Good,' Stevens said. 'No chance of a trap, I hope?'

'I doubt it,' I said. 'It's something the Arabs don't seem to go in for.'

'What's special about Lahej?' Stevens asked.

'It's practically on the border, and half the population are Yemeni refugees. They'd be on our side.'

'And you feel like going there then?'

'Why not? Better than hanging about in Aden.'

'Well don't get yourself killed,' Stevens said.

I was pleasantly surprised that it should be possible to take a taxi to Lahej, although I noted that the driver wore a gun, tucked into an armpit holster. We covered a few miles through Aden's slatternly outskirts before reaching an open road flanked by the muted outlines of the shipbuilding yards of prehistory. Lahej came rapidly into sight, surrounded by shining oases. The initial brilliance of its surroundings proved on closer approach to be something of a deception, for the town itself was subject to dust storms, its buildings being pallid with a greyish powder that stuck to its walls. Worst of all, the palms grouped by the hundreds in its open spaces released cascades of dust at fairly regular intervals when shaken by gusts of wind. A touch of fanaticism in its religious observances kept the citizens of Lahej more frequently at prayer than elsewhere in southern Arabia. They fasted, made donations to the poor, nurtured the sick, dressed without ostentation, played nothing but religious music, and had outlawed the gramophone. With all that they contrived surely to be the most friendly and companionable people it was possible to imagine. I had hardly released myself from the taxi when a passer-by pushed himself to the front of the small crowd that had gathered, and proceeded to offer me, using a simplified form of his language employed in conversation with foreigners or children, the hospitality of his home. I had already been warned of the almost embarrassing kindness of these people so I was able to excuse myself with a reasonable amount of grace. I then hastened to take refuge in one of the town's inns, in which Bedouin and their camels were lodged without distinction, before someone else, seeing me at a loose end, could implore me to become a guest in his house.

I was to spend two days in Lahej, enchanted by the rigidity of its customs. It was immediately clear that this was the great playground of the desert, and that these people of Bedouin origin remained Bedouin at heart and were the prisoners of pleasure. A man at the inn had told me, 'Parties go on all the time. We're addicts of them. If a man sells a few sheep he's likely to join with a friend and they hire a tent. It holds 200 people and they put it up in two days. Often it's for a wedding and everyone is invited. I could take you to a party now, and they'd rush to grab your hand and say "*Ahlan wa sahlan*" (Your very good health).'

The next day was a Friday, when the Sultan accompanied by his numerous family and the nobility of this minuscule realm walked in procession to pray in the mosque. I witnessed an inspiriting scene in which the Lahej army, composed of about one hundred British-trained soliders, marched both to the rhythm of native drummers and to the music of the only saxophone permitted by the religious authorities to be imported into the state.

In the evening I was invited to a party attended solely by men, at which the chewing of khat – the leaves of a mildly narcotic plant – was general, although this produced only a mild hilarity. A number of the guests had visited the barber earlier in the evening to have themselves cupped and a few arrived still wearing cows' horns covering gashes on various parts of their bodies. No disquiet was evident when, despite the illegality of photography, I used my spy camera to take pictures of this weird effect and other scenes likely to be of interest to Stevens. But my use of the camera – never seen and hardly even heard of – aroused interest and speculation in Lahej. 'I'm making pictures for the people back home', was my reason given, whether or not understood.

Lahej was within 300 miles of one of the greatest of

the earth's total deserts, but it had a temperate climate
and substantial rainfall. A guest at the party told me that
this was due to the mountain range to the north, the
beginnings of which were almost within walking distance. He offered to take me in his camel cart into these
mountains, and we set off together the next morning.
The distance was covered at a remarkable pace and
within two hours we found ourselves in a flowering
landscape.

We were now in the forbidden land of the Yemen,
passing through countryside watered by mountain
streams and covered with a profusion of green vegetation. It was too early in the year to enjoy the summer
maximum of this scene, but on all sides the aloes and
tamarisks, date palms and banana trees protruded from
among flowering aromatic shrubs. My friend, Said
Hamud, was a man of education who stressed the fact
that the climate of his land, although a part of Asia, was
more like that of a country lying far away to the north
by the waters of the Atlantic. In winter, he said, there
were stiff frosts within fifty miles of Lahej, although no
snowfalls. A little later, in season, I was told, these
mountain flanks would be clothed with jasmine, clematis
and wild briar, as well as – incredibly enough – with
bluebells and forget-me-nots. The more accessible valleys had already been cultivated with coffee beans, and
fruits of all kinds. My friend pointed out the monkeys in
the trees, and as a lover of birds I was delighted to
identify the hoopoe and the golden oriole. A pre-Islamic
Arab writer had said of this country that, 'Its inhabitants
are all hale and strong; sickness is rarely seen, there
are no poisonous plants or animals, nor blind persons,
nor fools, and the women are ever young. The climate

is like paradise, and one wears the same garment all
winter.'

What we had seen that morning explained the eagerness
of certain colonial powers to grab whatever they could
of this country, and it was fear of the colonialists, we
were later to learn, that had induced the Yemeni priest-
king Yahya to step up his military and spiritual
offensives. Ladislas claimed to have discovered that the
Imam had purchased 15,000 defective rifles from the
Polish government, and in the same week had trebled the
amount of compulsory public prayers. The kingdom's
postal services, he believed, had become a tool of
international spies. Thus Sir Bernard Reilly's letter on
our behalf was carried to the Yemen by one of Yahya's
personally appointed postmen, qualified not only to
deliver the mail but to preach in the mosque. Such were
the methods by which the King hoped to hold nemesis
at bay.

Aden had been neither East nor West, but a vigorous
hybrid of the both in which whatever differences that
existed were being vigorously chamfered away. Lahej
was an old-style Arabian town at its best – hospitable,
good-humoured and rather poor, with a fine collection
of old-fashioned prejudices that elsewhere had gone by
the board. Soft veils of dust hung over the buildings and
subdued the sun's rays to a bearable glow. This had been
an ancient tented town in which most of the population
now lived with reluctance in brick buildings forced upon
them by the authorities. It was noisy, for the drummers
of the Sultan's military band marched constantly up and
down through the narrow, echoing streets. Most people
possessed tents in memory of the good old days, and

occupied them whenever they could. 'You see,' said a native of the town with whom I struck up a conversation, 'we're all Bedouin at heart, and we like to be reminded of the way we lived.'

Perhaps the most extraordinary of my Arabian experiences was my meeting in Lahej with the celebrated outlaw, El Hadrami. He had turned up in the town a few days before my arrival and now basked in the prestige due in these parts to a man who had recently beheaded four of the King of the Yemen's guards sent to carry out his arrest.

El Hadrami's enormous fame permitted him to stage a procession of his own, timed on the Friday to follow the ritual of the Sultan's state visit to the mosque. I missed this demonstration of power, but later, on hearing that there was a journalist in the town, he ordered me to be ushered into his presence. He proved to be an immense and hugely muscular man wearing one of the new sports shirts recently imported from Europe, and with it a kilt. Spotting my camera, he ordered me to take a photograph of him, and drawing his enormous scimitar he slashed ferociously at the air. Several spectators had appeared in the background but were signalled by a movement of his index finger to withdraw. On such occasions El Hadrami was accustomed to invite a few leading citizens to lunch with him, and in this instance I was included.

The town's small central square was to be taken over for this purpose, but first a team of boys, furnished with brooms, filled the air with clouds of dust swept from the fronds of its palms. A rare local sucker-fish featured on the menu, for the first time that season, I was assured. It was in great demand, not on account of its insipid flavour, but in the belief that a little of what was considered its exceptional intelligence could be passed on to the consumer.

Silence, austerity and religious dictatorship – all the sworn enemies of pleasure – drove the most vigorous of the Yemen's sons to take refuge in the more congenial environment of the south, and after a short experience among these more relaxed Arabian scenes I formed a new theory of the Bedouin character. For these desert warriors, or ex-warriors, enjoyment was inseparable from the subtle pleasures of risk. Many of the citizens of Lahej had been born in or near the desert with eyes never able wholly to free themselves from imprinted vistas of sand. Boredom was thus their inheritance and in Lahej they demonstrated the lengths they would go to in search of excitement. This town was celebrated throughout southern Arabia for its rifle ranges where the bored shepherd escaping from the dunes did not shoot, but allowed himself to be shot. Finding it hard to believe what I'd been told about this I went to see for myself later on the Saturday. The target stood erect, hands over his eyes, and the marksman paid eight annas to shoot him with small darts at a distance of twenty yards, or a rupee to use a real bullet from which most of the gunpowder had been removed.

IV

In gathering information of the west coast with its flowers, trees, monkeys and exotic birds we made a discovery which Stevens rated as a useful find. Strangely enough, the road passing through these undisturbed surroundings had remained in a remarkable state of repair, despite its evident age. Said Hamud, my friend with the camel cart, had suggested that it was in such excellent condition largely because it had been unused for a century or more. Two or three hundred years back, he thought, it would have been essential to the conduct of hostilities between north and south. Nowadays all the business – and in consequence the disputes – of southern Arabia centred on the Gulf of Aden, where maritime traffic was all-important and what was left of the old roads were no longer used. There had been much talk of war in Lahej, but it would have been pointless, even disastrous, for the government of the Yemen to plan an attack down this ancient military highway, especially when it was known to possess only two armoured vehicles, both of them at that time out of use with engine trouble.

I had asked Said Hamud what Yahya's chances of success were should conflict break out. His reply was that the north would fare badly under the inevitable air-attacks against which it could offer no defence, but its army would be unbeatable in a defensive battle fought in the mountains. The Yemeni soldier survived rather than lived on a diet of dried figs and unleavened bread, and would be ready to fight to the death – which he would in any case regard as no more than the promotion of his soul.

Back in Aden after my short absence I sensed a change in the atmosphere of the place but some time passed before I decided that this was due to another influx of Italian soldiers. They were all officers, splendidly uniformed and courteous – if slightly aloof in their manner – but still perhaps a little dazzled by their recent victory in Abyssinia. They congregated in the lounges of the better hotels, bowing and smiling slightly when introduced to foreigners, but above all demonstrating a slight superiority, where their British counterparts were concerned, by never appearing to have had too much to drink. It was in the bar on the roof terrace of the Marina Hotel that I spotted Farago, who had been mysteriously absent for most of our stay. He was with an Italian, grinning broadly and gesticulating as he sometimes did. A second Italian officer joined the pair and the soldiers exchanged fascist salutes. At this point I moved behind a potted fern to give some thought to the possible implication of this scene.

That afternoon I located Farago in another part of the hotel and he told me that he had been to Djibouti – clearly at Stevens' behest. 'But why on earth Djibouti?' I asked. 'Isn't it French?' He grinned. 'These places change hands all the time,' he said.

It seemed better to change the subject. 'A lot of Italians about the place,' I suggested.

'I noticed that,' Farago laughed. 'They're quick off the mark. No Italian stays longer than he has to in Abyssinia. This must be like coming home to them. Just say "*Buon giorno*" and "*Come va?*" You'll find they're all right.'

'Any news of the permit?' I asked.

'None whatever. I can assure you that Sir Bernard Reilly has given it up as hopeless and so have I. All we have to do now is take the dhow to Hodeidah with a pocket full of fivers and talk to the immigration people there.' He laughed again – a sound in this case finishing in a whine like a dog's.

'When do we leave?'

'Impossible to say. The dhow people probably don't know themselves. Also they keep as quiet as possible until the last thing to trick the devil who preys on ships. All we can do is be ready with the luggage and sit down to wait until the omens are right. That's something that can take two or three days.'

'This sort of thing goes on all the time, I imagine?'

'All the time. Same as in Abyssinia. They had prayer groups there. You went down to the port and joined a group praying for a change in the wind, or whatever it was that was holding things up. A mullah led the prayers and collected his fees.'

'And they do that here?'

'Probably. We'll soon see.'

Later the news came through that the dhow would be leaving that night, and after a hurried take-off we arrived at the harbour in the early evening. Here, having delivered our gear to a crew member, we climbed aboard by a rope ladder and picked our way over piled-up boxes and bales in search of a place to put down our belongings. Most of the passengers had already settled in and scooped out nests for themselves among what could be shifted of the cargo. A few – perhaps braving the sea for the first time, and nervous in these surroundings – had apprehensively wrapped cloths around their mouths. I was told that this was in reaction to a local belief that at such moments of tension the spirit may suddenly endeavour to make its escape from the body. We had been given deck passages, and this came as a relief, for when we had first looked the dhow over we had noted a stagnant odour rising through the gangway from the depths of the ship.

V

The dhow's captain – the *nakhoda* – told us that he hoped to set sail in the early hours of the next day. But an hour after we had embarked a canoe came alongside, bringing a messenger from the city with an invitation for the dhow's crew and passengers to attend a wedding of a Hadrami family which had settled in Aden. This was instantly accepted and the *nakhoda* announced that work for that day was finished.

We were delighted to find ourselves included in the invitation. For one reason, we hoped that the marriage celebrations would afford us an excellent opportunity to get to know our future sailing companions. Of equal importance was our suspicion that, whatever the promises, we might still have several days on our hands before the dhow sailed. We were soon to discover that, as feared, sailing would be postponed due to exceptionally strong head winds. These winds, our new friends told us, were provided by Allah whenever there was a prospect of a good party. It would have been ill-mannered not to agree, and thus we made our way to the main entertainment, held in a large tent that had been put up on a waste space at the back of the town.

Inside, cushion-covered benches, forms and, above all, packing cases had been arranged in rows. This was the main gathering place for the 200 guests. Shortly before sunset the *nakhoda* and the crew of the dhow appeared. They lined up facing each other and to the rhythm of pipes and drums performed a sword dance. They pranced and gesticulated, advancing threateningly and retreating a number of times. Then, as the music and chanting reached a climax, they rushed to meet each other, leaping high in the air. The dances of the Hadrami, like most Arab performances, were violent and warlike. Swords had to be clashed as often as possible and if a party was going well – as in this case – someone would shoot out the lights.

When the dance was over, night had fallen, and we joined the guests, led by torchbearers, to the house where the bride's family lived, for the signing of the legal documents. An overflow sat down at tables that had been set out in the street, where they were served by members of the bride's family with coffee and sweets. Some, perhaps bored – even a little drunk – went to sleep, and these were approached by a soft-footed servant, who sprayed them with perfume. After about an hour had elapsed, the witnesses came out of the house. A basket filled with jasmine blossoms was passed round and when each guest had taken a handful, embraced each other and praised God, the party broke up for the night.

The wedding party was held next day in the great tent. Inevitably in southern Arabia, it was devoted to the chewing of khat – a drug guaranteed not to provoke argument or improper conduct of any kind. The guests stripped the leaves from their bundles of khat, pulled out their narghiles, refreshed themselves with mouthfuls of water and listened to the musicians. The host's two younger brothers were with him, as bridegrooms are never left unattended during the ceremonies, theoretically to protect them from evil spirits, but actually to avoid overindulgence.

The all-powerful barber-surgeon was master of ceremonies, and as each newcomer entered the tent the
barber played a few notes on a pipe and announced his
name. Guests went up to the dais, placed a gift of money
in the bowl set before the bridegroom and gave a small
coin to the barber in recognition of his services in
arranging the wedding. The low social standing of the
barber was curious in view of the essential services that
he performed. His most important function was that of
surgeon, and however fearsome the wounds he was
called in to treat, his services were preferred in this
Islamic community to those of physicians with medical
degrees – suspected in this society as sorcerers and
quacks. The barber in southern Arabia, like the sweeper
and the troubadour, was often recruited from the
depressed Subis, thought to be descendants of the
enslaved remnants of the Persian and Abyssinian
invaders of the Yemen. But because the bonds of caste
were loosely drawn, it sometimes happened that a
barber, escaping his destiny, would rise even to become
the governor of a province.

Morally and philosophically I did not think we had
much to offer of advantage to the East. But, generally
speaking, the ills of the body were not well understood
or capably treated. Bloodletting was the remedy for
most ailments. The traveller returning home after a long
journey made for the barber's parlour and had himself
slashed wherever he had felt pain while away. He sat
down in a chair, stripped to his loincloth, and the barber
cut into the areas that had given trouble. Then heated
cows' horns were cupped over the razor cuts and left
there as long as necessary.

* * *

Even khat may produce special effects when taken in abundance. Some of the guests began to sing quietly to the accompaniment of the *rebaba* and the violin of the musicians. Others fell into melancholy silence. Outside the tent the Hadrami seamen who had been chewing for hours on end laughed and clapped their hands and danced a kind of farandole in the torchlight. An unveiled Subi woman exorcized evil spirits with a prolonged and quavering howl. She was answered by the faint yapping of the pariah dogs that came down from the mountain slopes to devour the Parsee dead and to wander among the tombstones of the ancient Jewish cemetery. A few Yemeni Bedouin looked on with uneasy fascination. It was remembered in the Yemen that the Prophet, when he heard the music of pipes, had put his fingers in his ears, although recently Yahya had written a poem in music's praise, mentioning that its use promoted calm and the dutiful acceptance of the orders of those placed in authority.

Finally the feasting and the many delays were at an end. Two days later, half an hour before the appointed sailing time, we rowed out to the dhow and climbed the rope ladder again.

VI

Promptly at six o'clock the *nakhoda* raised his arms and gave an order. Several of the crew scrambled down to the bows and heaved the anchor up. Others grasped the rope and began to hoist the sail. This task, like the others on the dhow, was done to a rhythmic chant. A leader set the time by cries of '*He bab*', and, with each heave, the haulers roared all together, '*Allah karim*'. Some of the passengers went to help the crew with the sail. Before it was halfway up the mast, a chance breath of wind caught it and the dhow began to move slowly forward. Immediately, the helpers let go of the rope and clambered hastily to the sides to say goodbye to their friends. The air resounded with parting cries of 'God keep you', and 'Go in peace'.

It was a hot and airless evening. The burnished breast of the harbour curved gently with a sinuous movement from the depths and, in places, a vagrant breeze frosted its surface with changing designs. Momentarily the great triangular sail filled with wind, and strained billowing at the mast. Then just as suddenly it drained out and hung down loosely. We moved so slowly that looking at distant objects we seemed to be stationary. Only a gentle straining of timbers assured us that we were under way, and in the water thin streams of iridescence spread out and curled into rings over the gently heaving wake as the ship's sides disturbed the oiliness of the surface. Even the gull perched on the mast remained standing trance-like on one leg, and, as night drew close, stirred only to put its head under its wing.

While we were still a distance from the mouth of the harbour the sun began to roll down the sky, gilding the ship with yellow light. Some of the Yemeni who had previously wound cloths round their mouths now covered themselves completely. They believed that the rays of the setting sun were harmful and, for this reason, in the Yemeni capital, Sana'a, the houses had no ordinary glass windows facing west, but in their stead, round or oval apertures with panes of thin alabaster. These they called '*kamar*' (moon) on account of the moonlight effect they gave.

The sun reached the horizon. Silhouetted against the brilliant sky were the tall raked masts of the dhows that still lay between us and the open sea. The faint stir of urban noises reached us across the still water, rising above the soft splash of oars and the lapping of the water against our ship. At the sonorous '*azaan*' of the muezzin the *nakhoda* turned from the wheel and, facing east, raised a quavering voice in the call to salvation. Now the evening air came up over the bows, cleansing the ship of the staleness of sacking and dried fish and bilge. We clumsily moved the packing cases about to clear a little area of private space, and laid down our blankets. Most of the passengers who had come aboard with us lay huddled up asleep, but the Hadrami from the eastern end of the coast collected in the bows and began to sing the quavering songs of their country.

Packages of food had been left in our luggage and we were endeavouring to find them when our neighbour on the deck, father of a family of three, uttered what sounded like a cry of alarm. They had been busy with their supper, and now the man scrambled to his feet and came over smiling and bowing. What had become of our meal? he wanted to know. It was the first of a number of such embarrassing situations. These people, we were to discover, found it difficult to eat in the presence of others who were not eating without inviting them to share their meal.

We rummaged among our baggage, produced sandwiches, smiled and bowed and held them aloft. We had learned our first lesson, but it was a small problem that constantly recurred, and it took us a while to understand the complex routines of hospitality that governed life on board.

We soon became friends with our neighbours on the deck, and this quickly spread to the majority of the passengers and then to members of the crew. Possibly only the Western world tends to regard questioning of strangers as impolite. On the dhow curiosity was even a demonstration of good manners. A young man in temporary possession of a few square yards on the other side of the deck leapt to his feet at my approach, and smilingly said, 'Ask me something about myself.' I asked him whether he was married and what he did for a living, and scribbled his replies in my notebook. At this he was clearly gratified.

These Yemeni folk were strikingly handsome, with the refined features of a people locked away in their deserts for thousands of years. I was to notice that they seemed sometimes to respond to questions that were not asked, as if with our increasing familiarity they were mysteriously able to read my mind.

It was the practice on dhows like ours to carry a 'fortunate lady'. That night I was to catch my first glimpse of her. When the families were asleep the *nakhoda* summoned her for a tour of the deck, and as she stole past trailing an aroma of jasmine blossom I was astonished by how much beauty the faint gleam of her torch revealed in her face.

This young Somali girl was rarely mentioned in conversation. In Europe she would have been called a prostitute; here she was respectfully referred to as '*Sa Mabruka*' (the Fortunate One). A few days later I asked through a crew member if she would permit me to photograph her, to which she agreed. She proved to be as charming and beautiful as the sailor had suggested. But as she could not appear on deck I had to take the picture in the dim light of her windowless cabin; the result was poor.

The moon came up; the breeze died away, and we lay motionless on a sea that glistened with phosphorescence, white as a frost-flecked desert. The sail stretched above us like a dark wing, cancelling out the stars. Sometimes it gave a single flap and the mast creaked faintly. A stifling exhalation rose from the bowels of the ship and filled it to the brim, and the chanting of the Hadrami died away as if oppressed. Against the silence that followed could be heard the strong hum of mosquitoes, which the dhow harboured by the thousand. We soon found that protecting our exposed flesh from their torment meant unmaking our improvised beds and covering ourselves completely with our blankets.

The morning brought no freshness. Aching and sticky with heat we climbed to the side and looked around us. We were adrift in an expanse of steaming silk. Just over the stern, unexpectedly, the rocks of Aden were still imminent and huge after the night of travel. The harbour from which we had sailed the day before was only two or three miles away, but the short distance that separated us from the city's ash-heaps had wrought a change. The rocks had lost their sharp outlines and become pale and spectral, as if on the point of floating away.

As the sun rose higher, a canvas awning was unrolled and stretched over part of the ship to afford shade to the passengers. This was a doubtful blessing, because the awning held in the intolerable odour of staleness and decay which the sun seemed to scorch away wherever it was allowed to penetrate. We felt greatly tempted to cool ourselves by swimming in the sea around the ship, but on attempting to climb over the side, we were held back by the Arabs, who showed their alarm and pointed meaningfully at the water. We saw no sign of sharks, but the general nervousness impressed us and we abandoned the project.

For half the day we stayed motionless. Then a faint breeze began to blow from the shore, and to make the most of it the *nakhoda* had the sail changed for a larger one, and at last we moved again.

The Arabs began to prepare the main meal of the day. The cook was of slave origin and almost pure African in type. He was heavier, more thickset and more muscular than the average Arab, and his voice was deeper and more melodious. His face was pock-marked and twisted into an almost permanent grin. He prided himself on his professional artistry, and spent a great deal of time pounding and blending the ingredients for each meal. He filled in the intervals between his work by dancing and, as far as was possible, he used to dance even while the cooking went on. Up in the bows he kept an open fire on which he baked unleavened bread. The fire used to menace our lives by throwing out sparks which the breeze took and spread among the cargo. We were thankful that this was not especially flammable. Until recently, kerosene and petrol had often been carried by our dhow. This practice had been discontinued when four petrol-laden dhows in succession set sail from Aden for Madagascar and never reached their destinations.

VII

A feeling of unity and fellowship quickly sprang up. Chance had brought together on this ship some thirty men of different tribes and social classes, coming from places in Arabia as far apart as Athens is from London. Their bond was the common compulsion that had sent them out from their own people to travel to a far country. They were all intensely religious, and it was clear that practically all their actions were carried out in accordance with the precepts of the Koran. We found ourselves part of a community in which the issues of life were suddenly simplified and the essential virtues became of importance once again.

The moral atmosphere was perhaps similar to that of a medieval pilgrimage. Divisions between passengers and crew ceased to exist. On the rare occasions when there was work to be done everyone joined in, and at mealtimes all hands were dipped into the common dish. Arabs press food on those who eat with them. Ashore, sometimes, when we ate at table our host would become impatient of our mincing manners and, snatching our plates away, heap them with mutton and rice, strewing the food all over the table in his prodigality. The same spirit was present here, but we found *kishr* – a drink made from coffee husks – and unleavened bread like lead on the stomach.

Supreme command of all those gathered together on this ship was vested in the person of the *nakhoda*, who was tall, lean and grave. His beard was dyed red, but his eyebrows and eyelashes were long and white. His hands were so thin and long that they looked like the hands of a skeleton. His eyes were clouded and tired-looking, but he frequently screwed them up and shaded them with his arm, pointing out some elusive, half-obliterated landmark on the distant shore. Five times a day the *nakhoda* gave the call to prayer in his old, croaking voice. The first time he called '*Allah akbar*', the words came falteringly and could hardly be heard up in the bows, but he cleared his throat and started again and, by the time he reached the '*Haya ala'l falah*', his voice was strong. Besides the call to prayer, the *nakhoda* led the chanting at night, and sometimes when we were all resting he would tell a tale of the wit of some merry thief of old or the wisdom of a great king.

The *nakhoda* lived aft on a little platform from which the dhow was steered. This was as sacred to him and his officers as is the bridge to the captain of a ship. Out of respect it was usual to offer him the first piece of unleavened bread and to give him the first cup when the *kishr* was poured out. He always accepted it gravely, saying 'May God increase your blessing', or 'God be pleased with you'. When there was work to be done such as hoisting or changing sail, the *nakhoda* hauled on the rope with the rest, but he always maintained the dignity that became a man of his position. When something went wrong and damage was done, as was to happen later in the voyage, he did not raise his voice or wave his arms; instead he displayed the self-possession and restraint expected of an Arab gentlemen.

Our steersman was from Kuwait in the Persian Gulf. He was a young man who had once been a trainer of falcons and he still looked like one. He had also been a fisherman and he claimed to know the names of all birds and fishes. He used to point to the seabirds flying overhead, naming those that were good to eat. These, he said, he could attract by a certain call before flying his falcon against them. He told us of strange animals that his falcons had killed, including a bird that was larger than a man. He boasted that he possessed abnormal strength of vision – he used to point over the sea to towns and villages that remained invisible to us. To his credit it must be said that when we were on the lookout for a landmark or an island he was always the first to see it; often a man had to be sent up the mast to confirm the sighting.

Our sailors for the most part came from Bahrain, where they had originally been pearl fishers. They were not paid wages but received their food and a very small percentage on the sale of the cargo. One of them was keen to try his luck with the Italians in Abyssinia, and another had saved a little money and hoped to become a trader in Jeddah, where he had relatives. The experience they had gained as fishermen came in useful, for they trailed lines behind the dhow at certain times of the day, particularly towards the evening, to catch barracudas and rock cod.

As for our fellow passengers, these were people drawn from a variety of walks of life. As well as a restaurant owner with his family, we carried a man who sold masks and magical cures, a pearl merchant, and a circus performer who was to demonstrate how to ride a unicycle. Not everyone, however, travelled with such peaceable motives. On the deck just behind us sat a tribesman of the Beni Zaranik who was on his way to fight for what was left of free Abyssinia. These people lived in the coastal region of the Yemen, south of Hodeidah. Until a few years before they had been indomitable sea pirates and slavers, who had fought off invaders so successfully that they had always managed to retain their independence. Thus they were to prove one of the greatest impediments to Imam Yahya's campaign to rule the whole of the Yemen. Yahya's method of keeping these tribesmen in order was to take the sons of chiefs hostage, and of these he eventually had several thousands. But even with his hostages the system failed to work. Finally, in December 1929 Ahmed Seif-el-Islam, the Imam's son, had marched against them, and after a short but bloody war the Zaranik were exterminated.

Our Zaranik friend was not the only would-be soldier travelling with us. We also carried a Yemeni Bedouin without a penny to his name, but full of hope for the future. This Bedouin had been a shepherd, but his ambition was to become a military man in some country where soldiers wore imposing uniforms and did not have to buy their own rifles. After emigrating from the Yemen, he had worked for a short time as a coolie in Aden. There he had lived in one of the caves in the rocks to keep his expenses down. He had bought himself a shirt and an old black coat with his savings, with the idea of impressing future employees. He still darkened his eyelids, however, with antimony powder and bound his calves and his hair with sprigs of sweet basil.

One of the most likeable characters on the dhow was Sheikh Said. He was dark-skinned and slender with an expression of fierceness tempered with melancholy, and he spent much of the time standing in the bows staring out to sea, as if brooding over his troubles. When anyone approached him, however, natural courtesy made him cast off his moodiness and silence, and he smiled and held out his hand in greeting. Sheikh Said was from the remote interior of the Hadramawt, a country of blood feuds and civil war. It remained a land of fortified villages and towns, like the medieval Italian states of old, engaging in everlasting wars. These towns were built in fertile valleys and were often – unfortunately for them – within rifle shot of one another. Farmers would travel to their fields through networks of communicating trenches in order not to expose themselves to the eye of a sniper.

The sheikh spoke of feudal lords who built strong towers at strategic points from which they preyed upon the land. The townships employed mercenary troops and laid siege to each other with a few hundred men, an old canon and an occasional imported armoured car. It was these conditions, he told us, that had driven him from his country. As a sheikh he was debarred by custom from bearing arms in such conflicts, but he had been involved in a blood feud and then in a war in which he had chosen the losing side. A truce had been negotiated, but Sheikh Said, erring on the side of caution, had decided to emigrate.

Often to be found with Sheikh Said was an officer of the Ibn Saud's army who was returning home from a mission in the Hadramawt. He had brought along his bed, consisting of the usual framework and string netting, and lay on this most of the day reading passages from the Koran. Like the sheikh, he was lithe and slender, but his skin was as fair as a Scandinavian's. He was a man of education, and could write a few words of English. It was with his help, and with painstaking reference to dictionaries and our phrase book, that we

were able to carry on halting conversation with our
fellow travellers.

VIII

The more than leisurely progress of the dhow came as a
surprise. Occasionally a breeze tightened the sails, but
by the end of the first full day at sea we were to learn
that we had covered only ten miles, and by the next
morning we were in a flat calm. It was a situation
accepted almost with jubilation both by the male
passengers and several members of the crew. Many of
the passengers had brought fishing tackle along, in
readiness for forced inactivity, and now they baited their
hooks and lowered them into the sea. Within minutes
the first catch had been landed. The shores of the Red
Sea were devoid of human population, and the fishing
boats of Aden needed to go no further than the Gulf.
Thus the Red Sea abounded in fish.

To the fishing enthusiasts who travelled with us only a
few kinds were acceptable. Barracudas, which flourished
in these waters, were caught at intervals of a few minutes
without showing fight. But rock cod and big rays, the
other favoured catches, put up a great struggle. These
and a few lesser kinds free of suspicion were handed over
to the cook, the rest being immediately thrown back.
Occasionally a shark took the bait, usually snatching the
line from a surprised fisherman's hand.

At this moment I was made aware of a new facet of
Ladislas' personality. Someone had offered him a line to
join in the fishing, but this he refused with a shake of his

head. I was surprised. Why not join in with the others? His reply was to stagger me. This was a man who had spent his life as a witness and reporter of so many terrible scenes. 'I find fishing cruel,' he said, and I knew he meant just that.

After supper that evening we settled under a hurricane lamp for a discussion of the events of the day. Some reference to meals consumed in barbarous circumstances prompted me to mention an episode in *Abyssinia on the Eve*. There Ladislas had described a banquet, claimed to have been the biggest in national history, given by Haile Selassie on the eve of the outbreak of the war with Italy. Among those who took part were 2,000 accredited beggars and the main tent in which Ladislas found himself held 4,000 guests. As a matter of etiquette the Emperor himself and the dignitaries of the nation squatted on the ground with the rest of the invitees.

'And they actually threw food about the place?' Stevens asked.

'In a ritual way, yes. At the end of the tent newly slaughtered oxen were hung up and the servants cut off slices of the warm flesh and threw them to the guests.'

'To the Emperor as well?'

'Of course. A great shout went up when he caught a slice of meat and tore a strip off with his teeth. They drank a kind of alcohol called *tetsh*, and spat it out of the corners of their mouths so that it would mix with the blood.'

Next day the sea was as flat as ever, with all lines in the water and a massacre in process of so many beautiful fish. Several passengers including myself were on deck at first light, prey to a compulsion only to be satisfied by coming to terms with the dhow's 'place of ease'. This proved an atrocious experience when it could finally no longer be avoided. It was hard to believe that a contraption of this kind should be so difficult to gain access to. For technical reasons it swung loose on its ropes, thus partially freed from the wallowings of the ship; but for this reason only a calm sea permitted easy access and reduced feelings of extreme insecurity. Whatever the weather it was difficult for a European, buttoned up in his garments, to make use of the contrivance without loss of dignity, and in a period of storms which could last up to a week the problems involved became acute. We were to discover that in rough weather the victim would be lowered by the wallowing dhow at one moment into the cavernous belly of a wave, and thereafter hoisted high into the air over the cargo.

Three days later we were almost opposite the ancient town of Al Mukha, which once, under the name of Mocha, claimed to produce the world's finest coffee. We had to deliver two heavy beams for use in dhow-building to a small Yemeni village a day's sail further on. The *nakhoda*, who, so far as we were concerned, had remained somewhat aloof, suggested that we might care to go ashore. He warned us, however, not to get ourselves arrested, foreigners being rigorously excluded from even this minimally commercial area of the Yemen. Next morning the ship's boat was placed at our disposal for this interesting trip and we were put ashore on the beach, although, to be on the safe side, out of sight of the village itself.

It was the moment for several of our Arabs to play truant, slipping away quietly on an expedition we learned of only when they reappeared. It turned out that the exceptionally dense vegetation of a nearby wood provided cover for a large population of pigeons. The crews of passing dhows, who knew all about this, went pigeon-shooting there whenever they had an excuse to go ashore. Being almost pure white, the pigeons provided easy targets against the dark foliage, and although the Yemeni government sent the odd policeman to the area, these sporting expeditions had so far gone on with impunity.

In the village Ladislas and I listened to the popping of guns and an occasional faint shout of triumph. An hour passed before the sportsmen returned, some carrying pigeons, but all showing signs of alarm. It turned out that a member of the party had pushed his way a little further into the woods than the rest, and disappeared. The chances were that he had lost his way, but there was always the possibility that he had been captured and dragged off by a member of the Yemeni police. A horn blown on the dhow signified the *nakhoda*'s order for our return, and after an assurance that the villagers would send out a search party for the missing man we went down to wait for the boat. Within minutes we saw white sails spread at a half-dozen places as skiffs raced over to meet us. A villager explained that all the boys in them were slaves. Only slaves worked here, he said. He roared with laughter, because as we could see, he added, there was no work to be done. The slaves played tricks on each other, laughed and joked and pushed each other into the sea. It would have been hard in fact in this particular village to decide who was the slave and who was free.

IX

The *nakhoda* awaited us on our return. He was deeply concerned over the missing man, but he had disturbing news of his own. We were about to run into a storm of exceptional violence, he said, which would put us miles off course. We looked down at the pellucid green sea and watched tiny wavelets slapping at a boat tied up immediately below, waiting to be hauled aboard. It seemed hard to believe that a storm was coming, but the *nakhoda*, his usual calm if pessimistic self, warned us of what was about to happen. All baggage would have to be stowed away below deck and the *nakhoda* recommended that we take cover there, too, as soon as he gave us the signal. Male passengers, he warned us, might be forced to shelter in an area below normally reserved for females, and would be called upon to swear a religious oath not to molest them in any way. Second thoughts caused him to shake his head doubtfully. In our case, since we were not people of the Book – within reach of the salvation of Islam – such oaths would carry no weight. Were we, he wondered, prepared to change our faith for the period of the emergency? Playing for time, I said that it was a possibility to be considered.

We returned to the temporary sanctuary of our deck space, where the bad news was under discussion. One of our friends who had been in situations of this kind before assured us that anything was possible on the Red Sea. A few months ago a two-masted decked vessel bound for Jeddah had hit the south-west monsoon somewhere in this area and simply disappeared from sight.

Watching the western horizon we saw a powdery

vapour spread over the sky and slowly lift itself from the water. It brought with it a humming that could only be the roar of a distant storm. Five crew members were on deck busying themselves with the sails, but they were too late, for the first blast of the wind to reach us ripped the mainsail to shreds. At the last moment, the *nakhoda* swung the dhow around to face the tempest head on. Confronting it, the boat bowed very slightly, as if to a worthy adversary, before a mountainous wave smashed over its bows. A torrent of water rushed around us, over us and through our collection of struggling men, and the Koran held over us by the *nakhoda* was torn from his hands.

The storm waned, the sea calmed, and the *nakhoda* and his second-in-command went off with their lamps to inspect the damage, for by this time the loss of the mainsail had reduced our speed to barely two knots. The news that followed was bad. It would be impossible, we were told, with no mainsail, damage to the steering gear and a leak that threatened to get worse, to reach Hodeidah without assistance. Our remedy was to make for the island of Kamaran, where whatever repairs were required could be attended to. Kamaran was actually further off than Hodeidah, our eventual destination, but the wind favoured it, or so the *nakhoda* said.

The prospect filled passengers and crew alike with dismay. Kamaran – the Red Sea's only listed desert island – was seen as a place of supernatural terrors, of mysterious sickness and mania. Sailors shipwrecked there, even if physically undamaged, were said never to be the same again – they were prone to foolish behaviour and notably lost interest in their wives.

Assuring his crew that there was no alternative, the *nakhoda* closed his ears to their pleas.

We were in a paradise of nature that went unobserved. Long-winged terns encircled the boat, performing a kind of serial ballet before diving with infinite precision and grace to snatch fish from the waves. But the mood of the passengers, crammed together in appalling heat on a seemingly endless voyage, had changed. Little local feuds broke out among erstwhile good friends – often as they chased the small patches of shade which constantly shifted across the deck. There was an attempted suicide by a young man who, we learned, suffered from bouts of chronic depression. The *nakhoda* worried about the fate of the crew member who had disappeared at Al Mukha – it was feared he had been kidnapped, or even murdered. The fortunate lady's custom of appearing on deck at night to serenade favoured males came to an end when she was doused by infuriated wives with urine.

Two days later, as the sails snatched at the last flicker of breeze and fell limp, and as the belief spread that another night would be spent at sea, Ladislas groaned with despair. He loathed dhow journeys, he said, complaining of their terrible dependence upon the weather and their inevitable delays, the fetid breath of the bilges and the infernal creaking of timbers that robbed the night of sleep, the dire poverty of most of the passengers, and the religiosity of the *nakhodas*, who virtually enforced the attendance of travellers at prayers. Rex Stevens, who carried with him a small collection of classical books in readiness for such moments, passed Ladislas a volume of Smollett's *Travels*, but Ladislas put it aside. In a way boredom was his undoing – it was to

cause him to drop his guard and take me into his
confidence in matters which had previously been
excluded from our talks.

That afternoon, I was to hear for the first time that
Ladislas had had far closer contacts with the Italians in
Abyssinia than I had ever imagined. In an outburst of
candour he admitted that he had spent five months in
Rome as correspondent of the *London Sunday
Chronicle*. He had even been received by the Duce,
for whom he had been provided in advance with a
made-to-measure address of eighteen adulatory words.
Remarkably, too, Ladislas had confided to Stevens after
our first meeting that he would be particularly happy to
work with me as I looked like an Italian, and reminded
him physically of the fascist General Balbo with whom
he had been on exceptionally close terms.

These revelations were followed by an assurance that
he knew every Italian worth knowing in Aden, and that
although Aden had been promoted to the status of a
Crown Colony, Italian settlers – most of them in British
employ – surpassed in numbers, wealth and prestige
those of the resident English. The shadow of Mussolini,
Ladislas emphasized, had fallen across this great settlement of uprooted foreigners by the sea. The Aden press,
he told me, was manipulated by the Italians so as to
present the Abyssinian war as a one-off situation, with
Ethiopia remaining the single constituent of the Duce's
Roman Empire. But nothing was more relentless, said
Ladislas, than the Duce's determination to go ahead with
territorial acquisition. The small and weak Arab state of
the Yemen remained the only free nation in this corner
of the world, and little, said Ladislas, could be clearer
than the fact that it, too, would ultimately be snapped up

by one or other of the European powers. Our Arab friends on deck took this news with their characteristic fatalism. Whoever their rulers, they assured us, their situation was unlikely to change.

With the dhow in the doldrums it was an excellent time to fish, and while the children were left to quarrel happily among themselves our friends caught fish of all sizes, shapes and colours, forcing us into acceptance of the choicest prizes. Stevens withdrew with a book into a square yard of shade in search of the comforting unrealities of Suetonius. But Ladislas was not to be diverted from the magnificence of the new Roman Empire. Finding a passenger recently returned from Abyssinia, Ladislas questioned him on the quality of life under the Italians as compared with their Ethiopian slave masters, and the Arab told him there was absolutely no difference. In the afternoon's heat even the ship's timbers sweated gently, and here and there tiny scorpion-like creatures pushed their heads for a split second out of crannies in the blackened wood. Somewhere nearby a colony of cicadas clicked and hissed, and Ladislas wrapped a wet towel round his head.

Another mystery soon became clear. In the seven weeks Ladislas had been booked in at the Marina Hotel he had rarely been available to callers, and he was now quite happy to offer an explanation for these absences. 'I was away in Perim and Al Mukalla,' he said. 'Also Hadramawt. Ever been there? The name means "the Presence of Death". Understandably, too.'

'What made you go to all these places?' I asked.

'We were wasting our time in Aden. We were supposed to be going to the Yemen, but nothing happened. I knew people who could help us. I know the Sultan of Perim, and also the Sultan of Lahej.'

'We knew Sir Bernard Reilly. He did all he possibly could.'

'He didn't have the connections – people who count for something. The King of the Yemen has four wives and twenty-nine children. One of his nephews worked as a porter in our hotel. You would have done better to talk to him.'

'Well, there it is. We're committed to this now. We can only hope for the best.'

Years were to pass before the real explanation behind Ladislas Farago's mysterious journeys in southern Arabia appeared. His book of our travels, *The Riddle of Arabia*, was published in 1939 but, despite his fame as an author, it received little publicity and disappeared from the booksellers' windows within days of publication. The explanation generally offered was that it was in the course of reprinting, but the leading bookshop that had taken my order for a copy was never able to supply it. My attempts to find the book in the London Library proved fruitless. Finally, in 1999 a friend unearthed a copy for me and the puzzle of Farago's unexplained absences from Aden was solved.

In his book Farago describes how within days of our arrival in Aden he was lucky enough to meet a Monsieur Klar, a dealer in furs just back from Paris where he had attended an auction of hides and skins by the Hudson Bay Company. 'He gave me a letter in which it stated that I was a fur merchant and his representative. Without Monsieur Klar's letter I would never have reached the forbidden shores of the Yemen.' As the agent of an established trader all doors were open and a permit for the Yemen was immediately arranged. Travelling on the Portuguese steamer *Ayamonte*, he visited Hodeidah where he was comfortably housed and well looked after in the forbidden city. After completing whatever business it was that had taken him to the Yemen, a secret which he was never to reveal, he returned to Aden and checked in again at the Marina, this time in preparation for boarding the Arab dhow which was to take us all (in his case for the second time) to Hodeidah. This was the way, as he was to insist so often in our discussions, that operations of this kind were arranged.

X

Yard by yard the dhow edged forward through the night. Seven weak lamps lit the deck after nightfall, providing a gentle and soothing environment by comparison with that of the brash illumination of the day. The passengers, nevertheless, had wrapped scarves round their heads to protect them against the threat to their health of weak moonlight. Most had fallen asleep, and so they remained until the softest of winds picked up once again and Kamaran surfaced from the sea in the first flush of dawn.

Kamaran's romantic name, meaning 'two moons', was ascribed to the belief that under certain conditions the moon's reflection was visible in the water on both sides of the island at the same time. The first accounts of the island spoke of a race that had learned to harness cormorants in such a way as to carry human passengers in short aerial journeys over otherwise impassable territory. Subterranean galleries, said our guidebook, in which the population had taken refuge from piratical attacks still remained to be explored. Kamaran had been part of the kingdom of the Yemen until a few years before our arrival, when quite suddenly, and without explanation or published excuse, it had been taken under the control of a British administrator.

A freak of the dawn light revealed not desert sand as expected, but sparkling crystals by the thousand, heaped all along the edge of the tide. These, as we drifted in, separated into innumerable slivers of mother-of-pearl and shells tossed away by pearl fishermen, still asleep by their canoes in postures that mimicked death by exhaustion.

The *nakhoda* nodded and the anchor was dropped into the incomparably clear water. The families bustled into the boats to be taken ashore, while their menfolk waded through the bright mud and glittering nacreous rubbish to the beach. Smoke curled up as the first of the stoves was lit, the children chattered excitedly, the *nakhoda* prayed, and within minutes one of the pearl fishers raised himself with obvious reluctance and came scrambling into view. There was a primitive elegance about the scene. The supreme effort and the simplicity of the pearl fishermen's hard lives had left them with flat stomachs, protuberant ribcages and eyes brightened by peering into the depths. It was a breach of custom in all these isolated societies to ask questions, but we were to spend many days in Kamaran while our timbers were strengthened and our sails repaired, and answers were provided readily enough without questions being put. Nothing grew on the island, and in these pearl-fishing waters there were no fish except the occasional shark. 'If we eat nothing but oysters we cannot have children,' we were told by one of the wives. A husband had to take himself off to the mainland and live there for a month like a mainlander until his virility returned.

We sat down by a stove and struck up a conversation with one of the divers. 'We use a petrol can with a glass plate in its bottom,' he said. 'The shells are so large that only one at a time can be held in the hand and brought to the surface. Here we are all what they call shallow divers and we shall live to reach fifty years. Some of our friends are deep-sea divers. Their pearls are better than ours, but those divers will not last so long. At forty they're finished. It is all a matter of luck. A hundred shells were brought up yesterday, but of those only two produced pearls of reasonable size, and both were yellow and misshapen.'

Our surroundings were of the most austere beauty. The sea was dazzlingly green and vivid, and when – as we were later to discover – the dhows set sail for the fishing banks soon after daybreak, their keels could be seen so clearly through the water that they sometimes seemed to be floating out upon the air.

The British occupation of the island was still considered 'questionable', even by the press of the Crown Colony of Aden. Many maps still included it in the kingdom of the Yemen, and some even referred to it as Turkish. At its nearest point this long sliver of land – hardly more than a vast sandbank – was only some five miles from the coast, but its usurpation had aroused little concern or excitement in the Yemen. It had never been peopled except by a few transient pearl fishers. Its land was without water and produced nothing; and there were fewer hotter and drier areas in the world. Despite this, the British annexation had been carried out in a final flush of empire-building – a house was put up for an official 'administrator' who had in reality nothing to administrate, plus barracks for the handful of soldiers sent to support him in his duties.

XI

Kamaran's administrator at the time was Captain David Thompson, and as soon as we had recovered from our journey we set out to present ourselves at his headquarters, a mile or so away. The captain and his charming young wife were possibly the two loneliest people I had ever seen. Up until a few years before Thompson had been a military attaché at the British Embassy in Tehran, which he described with enthusiasm as one of the few cities of the Middle East where the good life was still to be found. The solution, Thompson told us, to the problem of their present isolation was to create occupation at all costs, and he lost no opportunity for keeping himself busy. With this objective in mind he had persuaded Aden to provide them with a Model T Ford and in this, despite the lack of roads and the presence of many areas of sinking sand, he was able to keep a benevolent eye on the island's people. These, he said, were no longer just a handful of pearl divers, but now included the members of a small community who had arrived on the scene a year ago. He had persuaded them to stay and taught them how best to fish away from the empty pearl-diving area.

Our visit to the Thompsons was a resounding success. Writing of this occasion in *The Riddle of Arabia*, Farago admitted that the days on the dhow had been some of the worst of his life, hardly less awful than the few days he had spent due to a police mistake in prison in Addis Ababa. (On his release he had received an apology from the Emperor himself.) By comparison with the long days and nights of the dhow the island, though 'a sea-lipped desert', 'came close to paradise' and the Thompsons' bungalow was upgraded to 'a mansion where I enjoyed refrigerated drink and all the comforts of an English country house'.

Farago had something in common with Thompson, for although they had not previously met he had been sent to Tehran by the *London Sunday Chronicle* to cover a difficult political situation while Thompson was there. Rex Stevens, too, was on home ground with his background in colonial government. Later, when Mrs Thompson joined us, Rex Stevens and her husband wandered off for a few words in confidence on colonial matters into a garden in which a single rosebush had struggled to survive under the protection of a small tent. This plant was regarded almost with reverence by the locals, who had seen no more by way of vegetation than a few blades of grass in all their lives. The Thompsons' serving girl even addressed it politely by the name of 'Ayesha'.

The *nakhoda* sent news up to the house that the repairs to the dhow would take some days, even weeks, to carry out. Thompson himself confirmed that he could not allow the dhow to leave until it was fully seaworthy once more. Nevertheless, the future was not wholly depressing, for a radio message came in that a steamer bound for Hodeidah was due to call in ten days' time. There was nothing to do but relax and occupy oneself in the meantime with whatever activity Kamaran might offer. For me it was to provide an opportunity to study the hard existence of the island's pearl divers, who were at the bottom of the human pyramid of one of the world's luxury trades.

Thompson, who I would have described as far from a social reformer, told me that, 'There is something about the pearl business, like the wealth mined from the earth – say, gold or oil – that seems to exclude mercy. These men are the sweated labourers of the sea.' The youngest of the divers were ten years of age and only a handful reached fifty – as my friend on the beach had told me – by which time their active life was at an end and they depended upon the charity of the community to survive. They were battened upon by a sequence of exploiters. A third of their catch became the property of the dhow owners who took them into deep waters. The price of what was left was negotiated by the agent the divers were compelled to employ and the pearl merchant – described by Thompson as a man of education and charm. What was extraordinary was that Thompson, who saw himself as a fair man, had been unable to abolish a traditional form of chicanery by which the negotiations between this pearl merchant and the divers' agent were carried on by secret hand-signs in which fraud was concealed. Eventually the pearls would be packed up and sent off to be sold in Bombay, at a price estimated by the administrator at some fifteen times that received by the men who risked their lives and ruined their health gathering them from the sea.

Thompson had done his best, he said, to rectify the worst of the abuses of the pearl-fishing trade. He had been promised a resident doctor to remedy a situation in which men, elsewhere accepted at their age as in the prime of life, were seen on the island as worn out. Above all, ferocious punishments had been abolished. Formerly a diver discovered attempting to dispose of a pearl secretly for his own profit had been given a can of water and set adrift in a canoe without oars. 'We're far more civilized now,' Thompson said. Nevertheless his own description of the pearl fisher's standard of living was that it was 'no higher than that of the labouring poor in the most downtrodden countries of Europe'.

Later on the conversation turned to the eccentric lives of those working Europeans – usually Englishmen – bold enough to take on rarely offered employment in Hodeidah, or the capital, Sana'a. A Britisher, the head of a foreign commercial undertaking in Hodeidah, had found himself in difficulties for importing a gramophone. This he was eventually allowed to play, but only in a room close to the shore where, with all windows closed, the music would be deadened by the sound of the waves. He was soon under investigation for teaching his servant to play tennis, which the Yemeni proposed to ban on the score of its being a dance and therefore atheistic.

In the Yemen, most human activities apart from those linked with actual survival were banned as 'against the will of God'. Apart from beheadings prescribed for all major crimes, thefts of petty objects or even food were punished by the amputation of a hand, and a whole range of minor punishments was inflicted for trivial offences seen as possibly against the wishes of the Almighty. It was illegal to sing, and even more to whistle, but retribution could also result from giving a horse a human name, walking backwards, climbing to the top of certain mountains and – seen in this case as a

reprehensible superstition – pointing at the full moon. In
Hodeidah and Sana'a watches could be worn, but only if
they were left unwound as ornaments. Harsh penalties
were imposed for smoking. The Britisher in Hodeidah
who was forced to close all his windows for playing
his gramophone distributed cigarettes among a group
of labourers who worked for him. The penalty for
smoking them in public turned out to be three months
in chains.

XII

Ten days later, as expected, a small cargo steamer, the
S.S. *Minho*, called in to pick us up, its only other
passenger being a gun-runner who boasted of the fact
that he had just sold the Yemeni a cargo of defective
weapons.

It seemed that Sir Bernard Reilly's appeals on our
behalf were at last to bear fruit, for when our ship
dropped anchor a quarter of a mile from the Yemeni
shore a reception party of notables came chugging out in
a motorboat to meet us. The newcomers, including
Hodeidah's remarkably bejewelled harbour-master,
climbed aboard, and Rex Stevens and I were told that
our party's permit to enter the country had been
granted, and that a house had been placed at our disposal
for our stay in Hodeidah. With that the visitors climbed
back into their boat and returned to the port. We settled
to await their return to be escorted to the promised
house, and a longish period of suspense ensued. After an
unexpectedly long delay it occurred to Stevens and
myself that some problem might have arisen over the

fact that Ladislas, who had been running a high temperature that morning, had not been present for our meeting with the Yemeni officials. 'His Majesty's permit granting your entry into our country,' the harbour-master had said, 'was for three persons. Where is the third?' It was explained to them that Ladislas was suffering from an attack of fever, which we took to be malaria. Stevens asked if there was a doctor in the port, and they shook their heads. There was none.

Two hours passed slowly with no sign of the return of our friends and doubt began to settle in our minds. Could something have gone wrong? Could Ladislas' absence from the interview have in some way aroused suspicions? There was no way of knowing. It now dawned upon me that Farago's sudden temperature had come as a surprise. He had passed some hours on the *Minho* before its departure from Kamaran, and during this time he had appeared normal in every way. But now suddenly he was complaining of a severe attack of malaria. He held out a thermometer which registered, he said, a temperature of 103 degrees. His face was twisted with anguish. It was impossible for him to talk to the Arabs, he insisted, because he was just about to be sick. A lurking doubt appeared in my mind as to whether Farago genuinely intended to go with us into the Yemen or whether, for some reason that remained wholly obscure, he did not. At this point I didn't, of course, know of the incredible subterfuge by which he alone had already crossed the frontier as a fur-trading agent of Monsieur Klar. At the time I thought it possible, as Captain Thompson had insisted, that as a newspaperman Ladislas would be automatically refused entry to the country, and that his non-appearance was a ruse to enable him to sneak by the officials. But Ladislas was not the only cause of our worries – next day the *Minho* would leave for Jeddah in Saudia Arabia. The Yemeni were supersensitive to the problem of foreign spies slipping past their frontier guards to explore the strength of their defences. Almost equally they went in fear of the plague – from which sick foreigners might turn out to be suffering. 'They are the victims,' as Thompson had put it, 'of faith, fanaticism and fear.'

That afternoon the harbour-master and his accompanying officials were back and our intuitions were confirmed. These men had discarded their masks of shallow amiability, and now proclaimed by their expressions that they saw through us. The harbour-master told us that His Highness, the King, had assumed we were there to sell them arms for the defence of their country. If we could offer the latest models of rifles and machine-guns for sale, His Majesty wished to be shown samples of them, but if our intention had been only to travel in his country and study its defences, our entry would be refused.

The turbaned dignitaries of the town solemnly arose from the chairs we had put out for them, and pressing our hands one by one they silently withdrew. They were returning, the harbour-master said, to obtain further instructions from His Majesty. Then he went. We knew from that time that only unofficial visits could be made to the Yemen.

Rex Stevens went back to tell the Portuguese ship's master that we would be ready, tides permitting, to put out at any time, and I was left alone on deck to take in a final view of the memorable front of Hodeidah – gateway to the Yemen.

This, like all the prospects of southern Arabia, was

different in many subtle ways from the models that had inspired it. In the great tidal wave of escapism that had followed the end of the First World War, rich Arabs from north Africa and the Yemen coast had sought temporary refuge from the asceticism of their lives by visits to such European playgrounds as the Côte d'Azure. Overcome with admiration they had strolled down such avenues of social display as the Promenade des Anglais at Nice, determined on their return to repeat these northern splendours in the sweltering tropics from which they so rarely emerged. But the environment they tried to replicate in Hodeidah was far removed from that of the Midi of France. It was charming in a wan sort of way, but it was different, and the final result reflected not the high-spirited self-indulgence of European holiday-makers but the inbred asceticism of Islam. The people of this coast had been trained from birth to draw their pleasures from fasting and prayer, and Hodeidah was the result of a temporary compromise between the two faiths. Decoration and architectural exuberance were restricted in these buildings to the top storeys 'because they were nearest to Heaven'. At street level they were plain and mute. There were doors but no windows.

I had been cautiously taking my last photographs of the scene when I noticed that a thin, ant-like stream of distant humans had come into view on the previously vacant and inanimate sea front. Putting my camera out of sight, but continuing to watch, I saw that these people soon branched off on to a narrow track that led eventually into the port. A few minutes passed and a black vehicle like a delivery van came up from the rear, pushing past the pedestrians that blocked its way. It turned off into a cleared space among a collection of hutments close to the water's edge, where it came to a halt. As the bystanders closed in, two uniformed men climbed down from the front seats, went back to open the rear doors and reached into the van. Moments later they reappeared with a man who was clearly a prisoner, since his arms were fastened behind his back.

The Portuguese captain was now at my side. Neither of us spoke while the guards hauled the prisoner into the centre of the cleared space, now kept empty by the arrival of two more guards. The two new arrivals took charge of the prisoner and forced him to his knees. 'This man has been brought here to die,' the captain said. 'Soon the executioner will come and cut off his head. If the people ask for him to die they will shout "*na'm*". If they are not wishing this they will make faces, and groan.'

'Why are they killing him? Is he a murderer?' I asked.

'No, he is not murdering. They are bringing him here because there are foreigners on the ships offshore and they wish them to see. This is the penalty for spying. The executioner will dance before he cuts this man's head off.'

'But why on earth should he dance?'

'It is custom. The executioner is dancing to give the people good heart. Before he strikes with the sword he will call out "*Ya akhuya*" which is meaning "Oh my brother", because he is sad for this man's death. Perhaps then he will sing. You must understand me these are not cruel people. All people in Hodeidah are kind. Only God is cruel.'

The crowd closed in and we caught a final glimpse of the executioner as he leapt and cavorted in his dance. Nothing more was seen of his scimitar but streaking reflections snatched from the sun. 'Listen to the crowd,' the captain said. 'Now they will call for the end.' But the only sound to reach us was a faint *ah*, whether of pleasure or despair – like a murmur to be heard distantly on some sporting occasion.

The captain shook his head. We turned and walked back over the deck and I moistened my dry lips. 'So now we will go to Jeddah,' he said, and the change in his voice suited his recall to duty.

'What is it like?' I asked.

'Well, it is still Arabia,' the captain said. 'At least we may say it is better than this.'

'That is certainly to be hoped.'

The captain said, 'In Hodeidah at this time there are three foreigners and all the Arab people are poor. Jeddah has many foreign people who are coming for a better climate, also because they may smoke, drink and maybe even fornicate with women in hotels. The Lord is everywhere in Hodeidah to punish men who do these things. In Jeddah, Almighty God is remaining in the mosque when the cruising ship is in port. That is important for Jeddah. That is why Jeddah is one rich city while Hodeidah is very poor.'

He turned away, then remembered our patient. 'So Mr Farago will be travelling to Jeddah with us?'

'Yes,' I said. 'When he next takes his temperature I'm sure it will be normal. He will travel with us as arranged.'

2001

54

THE SURVIVORS

THE DISCOVERY OF America by the Spanish initiated one of the most calamitous series of events and the most protracted human tragedy the world has ever known. Within a generation, all that remained of the grandiose civilizations of Central and South America were ruins and a wretched collection of plantation slaves, while to the north the impetus of conquest and extermination was only delayed. All the European newcomers were destroyers. The French demolished the nations of the Mississippi and the Gulf of Mexico. In Canada the British invented germ warfare by distributing blankets from a smallpox hospital among the tribes (a method favoured in Brazil to this day), while the freed American colonists pushed westwards behind a shield of treachery and massacre. The appalling fact is that most of the aboriginal inhabitants have been cleared from what amounts to one third of the world's surface, and it is perhaps even more depressing that the remnants should have been reduced, by and large, to destitution and cultural nothingness.

These processes of annihilation have been so thorough that it comes as a surprise to learn that in this continent, north of the Amazon, a major aboriginal group – the

Huichols of western Mexico – can have survived with their tribal structure, religion, traditions and art intact. Behind the bastion of the high sierra they were beyond the invaders' easy reach. Had there been gold or silver in the mountains, greed would have found a way to conquer them; but there was nothing in Huichol territory worth stealing, and there is no finer guerrilla country anywhere. The Huichols evaded the large military forces sent against them and defeated the small ones. Only in 1721, through a policy of blockade which cut them off from the sea and deprived them of salt, could they be induced to sign a treaty of peace. By the terms of this, five missions were to be established in tribal territory, but after a few years the missionaries gave up the struggle and went away. They had discovered that the Huichols were unsuitable material for conversion to Christianity.

Ten thousand Huichols have survived, and they have doubled their numbers since the turn of the twentieth century. One would expect this single exception to the rule of dwindling populations, apathy and degradation to be exceptional in every way – and exceptional the Huichols are. They live by hunting deer and growing a little maize – neither of them time-consuming occupations – and the huge surplus of leisure is devoted to the pursuit of the arts. They cover their clothing with elaborate embroidery and produce exquisite pre-Columbian objects in feathers, beads and coloured wools. All Huichol art is devotional. 'Everything we do in life,' the Huichol shaman-priest instructs the child, 'is for the glory of God. We praise him in the well-swept floor, the weeded field, the polished machete, the brilliant colours of the picture – of the embroidery. In these ways we pray for a long life and a good one.'

Most remarkable of the Huichol arts are the wool-paintings called *nearikas*, which have aroused much interest in Mexico of late, to the point of inspiring imitations of lamentable quality. *Nearikas* have been used from antiquity as votive offerings on all great occasions – such as at the birth of a child, when they are left at the mountain shrines – but until recently few have been seen outside museums. Some of the most striking are produced during the fiesta following the great peyote pilgrimage, which is a feature of the Huichol religion. The shamans, who have led their pilgrims across Mexico from the Sierra Madre to the sacred land of Wirikúta in the San Luis Potosi desert, eat the peyote cactus and create pictures inspired by their dreams, which are then left for the gods of the Sun, Fire and Water. Enlarged versions of such pictures are now being made and are sold in limited numbers to assist the Huichol economy, and last year (1969) in Guadalajara I saw an exhibition of them organized by Padre Ernesto Loéra of the Franciscan order.

What distinguished Huichol *nearikas* from any other Indian paintings I had seen was their exuberance; the feeling they gave of a lack of premeditation, of being the work of talented children. This impression turned out to be an illusion. Nothing in this art follows a mere decorative whim; every line, every curlicue, every blob of colour has its precise meaning. The tufts sprouting from the head of the manikin strutting along a path bordered with icicles and flowers are no mere fantasy, but the feathered ornaments representing antlers worn by the shaman in the exercise of his priestly functions.

To have omitted them would have been to deprive the picture of all significance. Most *nearikas* picture the legends of the Huichol race, or deal with the predicaments of the soul after death. They are always executed in brilliant colours because these are the colours of peyote visions, and they are considered so sacred that the Huichols working on them at Guadalajara do not permit strangers to watch them at work.

The pictures on view were largely the inspiration and occasionally the actual work of one remarkable man, the shaman Ramon Medina Silva, who lived for some years in a shack on the outskirts of the city near the shrine of the Virgin of Zapópan, a small-scale local version of Lourdes. The shrine attracts the sick from all parts of western Mexico and pilgrims whose complaints failed to respond to the visit sometimes consulted the nearby shaman, who had a wide reputation for treating psychosomatic disorders – particularly phobias. It was here that Padre Ernesto first met him, and a cordial relationship developed between the exponents of the two religions. Padre Ernesto seems to have raised no more objection to Ramon's shamanistic cures, achieved with spittle and incantation, than has the doctor in charge of the Huichol region. Both these enlightened men are happy to see the sick restored to health, whatever the means. Padre Ernesto, moreover, became enthusiastic about the shaman's artistic gifts, and encouraged him in these in every possible way – for example, by procuring wools of better quality than those within the shaman's reach.

Padre Ernesto had spent time with two recently established missions in the sierra, and it sounded as though their operations had been hardly more of a success than those built after the old treaty. But he was philosophic and indulgent, and however unresponsive to his ministrations the Huichols might have been, his enthusiasm for them kept breaking through.

He attributed the meagre harvest in souls to the Huichols' bolstering of their indigenous beliefs with the ritual use of peyote. It was a kind of drug-enforced theological brain-washing from which recovery or back-sliding – whichever way you looked at it – was virtually impossible. Peyote cults had spread in recent years, the padre said, to many of the Indian tribes of North America, but in reality this was a symptom of with-drawal and despair. The Huichols on the other hand were abstemious and disciplined, and they took their peyote like a dose of strong religious medicine. Peyote was a god, and by eating it they absorbed its divine force. The Huichols would have been horrified, he said, to hear themselves described as drug takers. He showed me a *nearika* by the shaman Ramon Medina warning of the terrible fate, the madness that overtook Huichols who allowed themselves to be induced by sorcerers to indulge in the hallucinogenic Jimson's weed (*datura*) – the methylated spirits of the demoralized Indian.

Then again, it had to be admitted that the gods of the Huichols were very close to them: cosy intimate figures from the family fireside, all of them seen and addressed as the nearest of relatives – Our Grandfather Fire; Our Mother Dove Girl, the Mother of Maize; Elder Brother Sacred Deer; Great Grandaddy Deer Tail. The padre thought that, by comparison, Christianity might seem abstract. In fact only one Christian saint – St Michael – had had any success, and he was accepted because his wings enabled the Huichols to identify him with the double-headed eagle god.

I told Padre Ernesto that I would very much like to
learn more about the Huichols by visiting them in their
tribal area, and he said that this was easy enough to do,
but I would have to arrange to go with a Franciscan friar
and stay at a mission, where I would be most welcome.
'Otherwise,' he said, 'you will be killed.' I thought that
he meant by bandits, but later I happened to meet a
Mexican who had been born in a village on the edge of
the sierra, and who said that some of the Huichols could
be trigger-happy at times. They had suffered from the
incursions of evildoers of all kinds, and a stranger
without obvious business was far more likely to be an
enemy than a friend.

Padre Ernesto said that all one had to do was to go to
the town of Tepic, in the State of Nayarit, ask at the
airfield for Padre Alberto Hernandez, and through him
charter the mission plane. This would fly to a landing
strip in the sierra, after which, he said, there would be a
short walk. I was to learn that the padre had fallen into a
habit – common among those who have had long
contact with Indians – of vagueness and understatement
in matters of time and distance. In these countries people
derive a huge and human satisfaction from telling others
what they believe they want to know, and a village
described as 'not far away' may be beyond a horizon of
mountains, while anything within several hours' trek is
often quite simply *aquicito* – 'more or less here'. The
alternative to the plane trip, and Padre Ernesto's 'short
walk' to follow it, was nine days on the back of a mule.

The opportunity to return to Mexico and see the
Huichols came early this year, and this time David
Montgomery went with me to take photographs. We flew

to Guadalajara for a last-minute briefing by Padre Ernesto, and from there we travelled to Tepic, down near the Pacific coast, by a Tres Estrellas bus – the heroic Mexican version of the North American Greyhound.

Early next day we went to look for Padre Alberto at the airfield. Here at last, after the anonymous cities, we found ourselves in a traditional Mexican landscape, illuminated by a bland morning sun. To the south, an eruption had dumped glittering coals on a horizon of lively greens. Eastwards a small volcano tilted its crater in our direction, and beyond it the Sierra Madre rose up in a gentle blue swell. Two Huichols had come to catch a plane that might be going somewhere next day, and they squatted among the gesticulating cactus, faces chiselled with noble indifference, absorbing time through their skin. Vultures were pinned here and there like black brooches on the sky, and presently there appeared among them the glittering insect that soon transformed itself into the mission's plane.

Padre Alberto drove up through the wash of the excitement created by this arrival, in a large American car. He came here every morning for an hour or two to supervise air cargoes flown into and out of the mission at Guadaloupe Ocotán; a neat, quick man in ordinary street clothes, with an important file of papers under his arm, who listened to what we had to tell him, but seemed unimpressed, and even wary.

Padre Ernesto, comfortably remote from such scenes of action, had been ready to promise anything. It happened that he was a talented photographer, and David, excited by his dramatic enlargements of masked and antlered dancers cavorting round a slaughtered bull, had hoped he would be able to get pictures of this kind.

The padre said that nothing was easier. If there didn't happen to be a fiesta on wherever we happened to find ourselves in Huichol country, what was wrong with manufacturing one? 'Buy a bull,' he said, 'and get them to sacrifice it.' It was clear that his attitude towards the performance of such pagan rites was a liberal one.

We mentioned this suggestion now to Padre Alberto, and he shot us an austere glance. A slight chilling of the atmosphere could be detected. 'Such sacrifices,' he said, 'are strictly reserved for ceremonial occasions. I'm afraid that at the moment you would find little to interest you in Guadaloupe Ocotán.' He then exploded his bombshell. The mission's plane was too busy carrying urgent cargoes to take us to the sierra. If we still insisted on going, all he could suggest was that we chartered a twin-engined Beechcraft belonging to a local company. This could fly us further into the sierra to San Andres, where there was the only airstrip it could use, and from San Andres we could walk to Santa Clara where the Order had their second mission, and where they would be able to put us up. It would be expensive, and – it had to be pointed out – chancy, because the weather at the moment was tricky, with high winds, so that even if the Beechcraft could fly us in, there was no telling how long it might be before it could pick us up.

At this point it began to sound to us like nine days on the mules after all, but soon afterwards there was better news. The padre, who had rushed off to inspect packages, give instructions and sign papers, was back to tell us that the Beechcraft would be making the flight to San Andres in any case next morning. This was a Friday, and on the Sunday – which was not normally a working day – the mission's Cessna could be chartered to fly in and pick us up at Santa Clara, where there was a small airstrip it could use.

This solution we accepted with huge relief, although San Andres was twice as far away as Guadaloupe Ocotán, and we had heard there were fewer Indians there. A suspicion lingered that the padre might have decided that this was the best way of getting rid of us. Why – it was hard to say. Writers and photographers could be a nuisance in off-the-beaten-track places like this. A Mexican magazine had just published unflattering photographs of the Coras, taken by a visiting journalist, as a result of which the outraged Indians had barred whites from the Cora tribal area of the sierra. As soon as it was quite clear that there was no chance of our turning up at Padre Alberto's mission, the atmosphere cleared and we parted the best of friends.

After leaving Padre Alberto, we made a courtesy call on Dr Ramos, of the Instituto Indigenista, whom we found seated at his desk beneath a fine *nearika* of the doubled-headed eagle. On our enquiring whether this was the work of the shaman Ramon Medina, the director said that it was, and added that the shaman happened to be in Tepic at that time. He thought he might agree to meet us and allow himself to be photographed. This was an almost incredible piece of luck because the last time Ramon Medina had been heard of in Mexico City he had been living on his family rancho, somewhere in the remote sierra. A tentative appointment was fixed at the Instituto's office for four that afternoon.

The shaman arrived punctually; a remarkable figure even in Tepic, where there were many Indians in the street, and not a few of them in bizarre regalia. He was a man of about forty, with a small, brown, smiling face and penetrating eyes and, in his cotton shirt and trousers embroidered with deer, eagles and jaguars, and his wide hat decorated with coloured wools and fringed with pendant ornaments, he dominated the discreet environment of the Instituto's office.

Fears that he might not wish to be photographed were soon dispelled. Regarded by his countrymen on ritual occasions as an incarnation of the Fire God, the shaman was remote from small-scale intolerance, and he allowed himself, endlessly benign, to be studied from angle to angle, and shifted from position to position, while the shutter of David's camera clicked interminably.

It was a huge advantage that although he spoke no English, his Spanish was slow and precise, as if learned late in life, and there were no problems in understanding each other. When we told him of our plans, he shook his head. It would be impossible to see anything of the lives of the Huichols if we went by ourselves. They came down into their five villages only for ceremonial purposes, living otherwise in isolated ranchos throughout the sierra, which no stranger would ever find. We told him that we proposed to make the attempt, whatever happened, and the shaman said: 'In that case, perhaps you would like me to come with you.' This we assumed at first to be a piece of Indian politeness, like the offer of a well-bred Spaniard to accompany you when you stop him to ask the way. It was difficult to believe that the shaman really meant what he said, but he did. He was as free as the air to come and go where and when he pleased, he said. We could leave at that moment if we liked.

Disconcerted a little by this almost inhuman display of independence, we finally agreed to pick the shaman up next morning, and at 5.30 we went in a taxi to find him in a glum little street on the outskirts of the town, where all his neighbours were waiting with their lamps lit to see him off.

The plane should have left at six, but by the time it lumbered down the runway and bumped into the air towards the sierra the sun was well up. Besides the three of us, there were two other passengers: a Huichol and his exceedingly pretty wife, aged about fourteen. She had the small-boned, elegant face of an Andalusian dancer, without mongoloid traits, but her cheeks were brilliantly rouged in Indian style. At the airport she had sat apart, her back to her husband, in demure Huichol fashion, but now protocol had collapsed under the strain of the experience, and she had buried her face in his neck.

Through the scratched and misted windows of the Beechcraft, a dramatic landscape had been spread beneath us, rocking gently as the air currents buffeted the plane. We stared down into the green baize-lined crater of the small volcano, and not far from it – despite the fact that Nayarit is supposed to be devoid of archaeological interest – a neat construction of concentric rings that was unmistakably an ancient pyramid appeared and slid away. Ahead, the sierra threw itself in grey waves against the horizon, and the Beechcraft thundered towards them. After my years of air travel in jets, it seemed hardly to move but to lie suspended, flinching and shuddering in each trough of the mountains before the struggle up to clear the next shattered Crusaders' castle of rock, with a hundred feet or so to spare. At these moments of maximum effort the fuselage flexed gently, and the pilot reached out to make an adjustment here or tighten a wingnut there. The Rio Chapalanga, drawn in its gorges like a flourish under a signature, appeared and vanished again. The shaman, remote from preoccupations and perils, said that the fishing in this river was good, and he pointed with relish to locked-away valleys where jaguars abounded.

At last a narrow tongue of tableland came into sight across a low precipice, with a patch of fabric among its trees that was the landing strip, and we banked to come in and touch down.

We climbed down from the plane and looked round us. We were in a clearing of a forest of sparsely planted oaks; bromeliads knotted with their thin daggers of blossom among their branches. Harsh sunshine shattered itself on facets of jade and ice on the rocks beyond the runway, and a freezing wind hissed down. Saying something about worsening conditions, the pilot clambered back and made haste to take off. A group of Huichols with painted faces, squatting in expressionless contemplation of this miracle, got up and trotted away into the trees.

We were carrying a tremendous load of cameras and tinned foods, and the problem that now faced us was how to struggle under this weight to the mission, which the shaman Ramon assured us with a smile that only inspired doubt was only one hour away. Two apathetic and fragile-looking Huichol women now appeared, as if from a hole in the ground, and the shaman immediately enlisted them as porters.

The loads were distributed, the shaman taking the heaviest package, and we were about to make a start when he asked us whether we had brought arms. He seemed surprised that we had not. Slung over his shoulder was a splendidly ornamented satchel, and from this he took a 9mm pearl-handled Star automatic pistol, which he stuck in his belt. Had he known we were unarmed, he said, he would have brought his Luger as well, and perhaps his bow. I asked why, and the shaman said we might have shot a deer. His explanation surprised me, because I had read somewhere that the deer was regarded by the Huichols as their totemic ancestor, as well as a minor deity. The ordinary people, I had read, ate deer flesh on the occasions of their major feasts, but it was taboo to their shamans. Ramon later admitted that this was so, and that in his case the killing of a deer would involve a complete magic dislocation, which would inevitably bring about his instant death.

We now set out over a narrow trail up a gradient leading to low peaks ahead, the shaman leading the way, followed by David and myself, and then, at a respectful distance, the two Huichol women with a valise apiece suspended from cords tied across their foreheads. The landscape had become delicately artificial, a piece of chinoiserie carved from ivory and shell for the amusement of the court of Versailles, and the shaman slipping ahead of us through the trees looked like a tartar from a Russian ballet, or an ornamented Polovtsian, rather than the Indian he was. There was no undergrowth in the forest, and great boulders had been artfully arranged among the beautifully distorted firs and oaks. Clouded blue water trickled through a valley over porcelain rocks, which Ramon told us were full of opals. A macaw, indigo and orange, flashed from the high branches and Ramon held it for a moment with a strange ventriloquist's whistle. There were gay, squawking birds everywhere, and a few years ago, the shaman said, we would have seen wolves along the trail, and might even have had the luck to run into a bear, or a jaguar; but of late more and more Huichols had come to own .22 rifles, and the animals had withdrawn further into the sierra.

An hour passed and then two hours, and the track became narrower, steeper and more cluttered with boulders. At one point we passed along the edge of a slope looking down over a gorge that was a small version of the Grand Canyon in dour greens, and the women who had been calling to the shaman came up and pointed to a Huichol rancho – the first we had seen – on a hillside a mile or so away. The shaman's face changed, and when I asked him what was the matter he said the rancho had been attacked by bandits who were active in the neighbourhood – although in this case the attackers had been driven off. The day was hot now; here we rested, and Ramon, after offering a prayer to the rain god, went down on his hands and knees, blew the scum from the surface of a marshy puddle that had been there since the last rainy season, and drank deeply.

Three-and-a-half hours after setting out from the airstrip we finally came in sight of the mission. It had been eight miles over hard terrain, and only the shaman showed no signs of fatigue. Coming down the path to the compound we met Padre Joaquin, the Franciscan in charge, who had just arrived in the mission's Cessna, and we were a little surprised to learn that he had been the only passenger. Our reception seemed less enthusiastic than Padre Ernesto had led us to hope that it might be, and no great intuitive effort was called for to conclude that this was probably the last man in the world to speak to about organizing a pagan fiesta. Ramon had suddenly fallen back and was invisible among the trees, but the father had certainly caught sight of him and it occurred to us that the appearance in these surroundings of a shaman in all his Stone Age trappings might not have been altogether welcome.

The padre was a man of few words, and little was said until we crossed a stream in which a large, battered metal object lay half-submerged. He told us that this was the remains of the mission's workshop, which the Huichols had burned down two years before. Speaking with some emphasis, he added: 'They were hostile to us at that time.'

To further conversational efforts he replied briefly. The primary function of the mission, he said, was to educate Huichol children, and at that moment they had some sixty pupils of both sexes – all of them boarders, because their family ranchos were too far away for them to return home each day. No charge was made for instruction or board. The children had the afternoon free from study, so we would not see many of them about. He made no offer to show us the mission, but wanted to be quite sure that there was no mistake about the arrangements for our departure. The plane would come on Sunday morning – early, he said, to avoid the high winds. He showed us to the hut, on the edge of the compound, where we were to sleep and quickly made an excuse and left us. A suspicion that he would not be sorry to see the back of us was beginning to grow in our minds.

Later, sitting with the shaman among the trees in this refined landscape, while woodpeckers with fiery crests scuttled up and down the trunks all round, I made a cautious approach to the topic of the conflict between the two religions, and Ramon set forth his views on the subject with frankness and authority.

The religious instruction the Huichol children received at the mission, he said, was unimportant. A Huichol soul always remained one and could not be 'caught' by the Christians. Whatever the shortcomings, the errors, or the backsliding of this life, he, the shaman, would come for it at death. He would release it from the thorn on which it had been impaled for its sins, draw it through the purifying fires and guide it past the animals that menaced it at the gates of the underworld. Freeing it after its sojourn in the land of the dead, he would escort it on part of its journey to the sun, and if after five years it craved to return to earth he would build the grass shrine to be placed in the family house, where it would live on in its earthbound form as a rock crystal.

Warming to his theme, his voice pitched in a high incantatory drone, the shaman described the endless after-death saga of the imperishable Huichol soul. And this was the charge that he laid against the missions. Baffled in their attempt to convert the Huichol, their policy was to capture his children by turning them into *mestizos* through their parents' intermarriage; the boys and girls at the mission, he said, would be encouraged to marry out of their tribe. The children of such marriages would be baptized, and they would be lost to the Huichol race.

A little later the Vespers bell rang, and the *mestizos* came riding down the trails to attend the service; men, as Lorca would have said, with their mouths full of flints, slender and saturnine, and dressed in cowboy style with big sombreros and leather chaps. They doffed their hats as they passed, and the shaman gave them the easy smile that hid an implacable antagonism. These men were nothing. They had the souls of the mules they rode, he said. As an example of what they were capable of, he said that they bought and sold land – the most irreligious of all acts in the eyes of a communistic Huichol.

The image of proselytizing Christianity as seen through an Indian's eye was hard to refute. The record of the missions in the Americas is at best dismal, and at worst makes painful reading indeed, and, whatever the purity of their motives, the Franciscans must share the blame for the degeneration of the Indians of California, and for their final disappearance from the scene. Christianity has too often been administered as a sedative – something as deadly in practice as raw alcohol – designed to keep the fighting Indian quiet and persuade him to turn the other cheek while his destruction was being prepared. At Santa Clara, however, the mission offered a phenomenon that was new, at least to me; the spectacle of love, not only preached but put into practice. Here at last, and for the first time, I saw Indians as the early explorers and colonizers saw them, before the assassinations began; gentle, friendly, and brimming over with laughter.

It was early evening with a resplendent sky full of toucans and parakeets, and soft lemon light. The girls had finished their domestic chores, and the boys had come down from the forests dragging wood on sledges for the fires; now they collected in little groups, curious and smiling round our hut. They were of all the ages of childhood. Some of them had the faces of little Eskimos, while others could have been European gypsies; and yet other faces were totally and unmistakably Mexican from the temple bas reliefs in the ruined cities of the south. What astonished me again was that the Franciscans had allowed them to dress in pure Indian style, with all the

Indian gods embroidered across well-laundered clothing. Some of the boys had guitars and Huichol violins, and it seemed that we were to be serenaded, but despite the encouragement of the girls, who kept up a vigorous pentatonic humming, the musicians turned out to be too shy to entertain us with more than a few strummed bars.

The shaman sat apart, writing with a ball-point pen in his notebook. Although illiterate by the standards of the West, he recorded the day's events and the flow of his own inspiration, just as a pre-Columbian Aztec might have done, in a series of vigorous ideographs. Now he interrupted his writing to criticize the feebleness of the musical performance. He was opposed to witchcraft but this was one field in which the end justified the means. A Huichol parent who wanted his son to be a first-class musician normally sent him in the charge of an enchanter to the place where the magic *arbol del viento* grew. For three days and three nights the pupil would sit and listen to the wind in the branches, and then he played. When he returned home not a violinist could equal him. What was that tune that one of the older boys was scratching out so feebly? I told him it was 'Silent Night'.

David had had the splendid notion of bringing a Polaroid camera along to help break the ice on such occasions, and now he performed the important magic act of producing snapshots of a number of these beautiful children. The impact of instant photography was interesting to watch. Tension mounted with the stripping of the paper from the print and the laughter died from the faces leaving pure awe. The subject, clutching his or her portrait, would back away with it, trembling with excitement, to find a quiet place to be alone, while others crowded to the front to submit themselves to the same shattering experience. From this time on the children rarely left us alone.

In the meantime the shaman had found two adult Huichols at work on the foundations of a building on the outskirts of the compound, and had gone off to enquire from them what were the possibilities of our witnessing any interesting ceremonies in this part of the sierra. He had already assured us that they were slight. People who live off the land, the world over, can best find the resources and the spare time for celebrating when the harvests are newly in – and in the Sierra Madre this is in the months of October and November. After that, food supplies begin slowly to diminish, and the arid season arrives when no rain falls in the mountains and the grass withers away. The Huichols, always semi-nomadic, leave the ranchos where they cultivate their patches of maize and squash, and take their few animals to explore the remote valleys in search of pasture. In bad seasons – and this had been one – the maize soon runs out, and the family eats once a day, and then every second day, and the active young men and women leave their families and trek down to the Pacific coastline to grow a cash crop of tobacco.

Ramon had shown himself as anxious as we were that we should see all we could of the life of his people, and in our presence and without the slightest embarrassment he had prayed long and earnestly to the Sun god for the success of our journey. Now, coming back, he announced that his prayers had been answered. Unpropitious though the season was, it turned out that the people living within two days of the village of San

Andres – near the airstrip where we had landed – would hold a fiesta there that Sunday, with archery, music performed on ancient instruments, dancing, great quantities of *tesguiño* (ceremonial beer) and possibly a bull-sacrifice, if an animal could be spared. We pointed out that we were bound to miss all this, as the mission plane was due to fly in early on the Sunday morning to take us off. For a moment the shaman's face fell, but he brightened to assure us that even if we missed the fiesta itself, there would be plenty to interest us in the preparations for it, which would certainly begin on the previous day.

He now produced a disquieting piece of information. He had just learned that four days before – on the Monday – bandits had broken into a Huichol rancho just out of sight in the fold of the hills from where we stood, robbed the owner, and then murdered him by hanging.

The degree of deliberation that had gone into the atrocity shocked us. To hang a man seemed more barbarous than to shoot or knife him – but why kill at all? I had been told that bandits were still common enough off the beaten track in Mexico, but had always assumed that, in an encounter with them, to offer no resistance would be to ensure that one's life would be spared. In the sierra, the shaman said, bandits were not like that. They were cruel men. They robbed and they killed, and hanging – which called for practice and expertise – was the preferred method. I now recalled Padre Ernesto's story of coming across a woman hanging from a tree on one of his photographic jaunts, and I also remembered that besides his Hasselblad camera he always carried a .306 repeating rifle.

It came as a pleasant surprise when a little later one of the boys came to summon us to supper. The shaman excused himself, saying that he never took food after midday, and we followed the boy to a deserted dining hall where he served us bowlfuls of atole – a sweet, corn-flour gruel – followed by tortillas and bean-stew; all of it delicious.

The night was cold and we slept in our clothes under what we could find in the way of blankets, drowsing off in the end to a soporific background mutter of the shaman's prayers. After three in the morning the strengthening chill made it impossible to sleep any longer. This was the hour, too, when the Huichol day starts, and we could hear Ramon shuffling about in the darkness, and finally the door opened and closed behind him as he went out. At about four, activity outside became general, and Huichol children, irrepressibly musical, came and went about the morning's business, strumming their guitars and playing their Huichol violins.

At about six, we ourselves decided to face the gelid air and dragged ourselves stiffly up the hillside in the direction of a fire. Here we found the shaman, who had been joined by a semi-circle of *mestizos* – silent and motionless pyramids of blankets capped by their immense crammed-down sombreros, so that nothing showed of them but their eyes and the toecaps of elegant boots. Presently we were joined by some of the boys who had been for a swim in the freezing river. Ramon found evidence of self-indulgence in this. Three in the morning was the time to take one's dip, not dawn. He mentioned that this was the habit of any woman worthy of consideration. Such dousings fostered the natural sexual coldness that the Huichols appreciated in their womenfolk. He added the interesting information that any Huichol who had intercourse more frequently than once every ten or fifteen days was regarded as a debauchee, and the ideal of sexual conduct had been established by the tribe's divine ancestor, the deer, who limited sexual activity to a brief yearly season. Later, when the *mestizos* had gone, he added the opinion that apart from the fact that they had no souls, the main cause of their inferiority was their over-indulgence in intercourse, by which they wasted their blood.

The sun came up with reluctance, although assisted by the shaman's prayers. David and I went off for more tortillas with atole, and the shaman, who now admitted that religious scruples prevented him from eating mission food, allowed himself to be tempted by a packet of the rich tea biscuits David found indispensable to travel.

We then set out on the hard walk back to San Andres – this time travelling light, except for the shaman who had volunteered to carry the cameras. The day had made a brilliant start as we walked through glades patterned with minute scarlet flowers, among small shellbursts of sunshine and rocks and water. Once again we stopped to rest and look down over the frenzied landscape of the Nautla Gorge, where the Huichol idols are stored in the cave of Te Kata. The cave, Padre Ernesto had said – tempting us to further adventure – was only a half-day by mule from Santa Clara, and no white man had ever been there. It was a temptation we had to resist.

A little further on, as the terrain levelled out, we saw a Huichol coming up towards us through the trees, but after a moment he left the trail and appeared to be making a detour to avoid us. The shaman called to him when he came level, although by this time he was a hundred yards away. He stopped and we saw that he was carrying a yellow-painted rifle. There was a short interchange in Huichol, after which the man went on, and the shaman stood watching him until he was out of sight. He seemed subdued. 'There's to be no fiesta in San Andres after all,' he said.

We walked on for another few minutes. Suddenly Ramon stopped and held us back. Two branches had been laid to cross over the trail, and the shaman bent down to study them and warned us not to pass. He then announced that this was a *travesía* – a matter of witchcraft – and the intention was to warn off visitors to the village. Picking the branches up, he threw them into the air and blew after them. Then he wiped his hands as carefully as if they had been contaminated with radioactive matter. He asked if we still wanted to go on, adding that he had dealt with the spell. We told him that we did.

A *mestizo* now appeared, riding towards us, and the shaman barred his path. This man looked like an extra from the film *Viva Zapata*, with narrowed, sleepy eyelids, a few hairs drooping from the corners of his mouth, and a heavy pistol sticking out of his saddle bag. The shaman started a stern questioning in Spanish, and the *mestizo*, having to explain his presence there, began to look alarmed.

He was going to Jesus Maria, he said, to try to buy cattle. He couldn't say from whom. There was a man there whose name might have been Pedro, or Juan. He couldn't remember. Nor could he supply the name of the *Tatouan* (governor) of Jesus Maria. The shaman asked him if he had any associates in this district, and he said he was the partner of a Señor Adolfo Castañera. He fidgeted and sweated while Ramon interrogated him, his hand on the butt of his gun. In the end he was allowed to go. 'He is one of those who murdered the Huichol,' Ramon said. It seemed impossible to ask him how he knew, and in any case there was an imprecision in the charge permitted by a certain woolliness of language. '*Uno de esos*' – it might have meant that the man himself had been among the killers, or that he was of the kind that committed such murders.

San Andres came into sight beyond the airstrip, and when we arrived there was little doubt that any intended fiesta had been called off. The village comprised about fifteen stone-built windowless houses, spaced round a wide square, and both the buildings themselves and the earth they stood on were a deep and lugubrious red. In the centre of the square stood a shrine and by it a post, to which arrows had nailed three small faded garlands of orchid flowers. This, we were later informed, was the post to which deflowerers of virgins were tied to be flogged, and the three crowns symbolized cases of ravished virginity.

At the moment of our arrival the only human form in sight was a single Huichol sprawled half asleep against the veranda of what seemed to be the village's principle building. This, Ramon told us, was the *topiri* – the police officer – and he pointed out the insignia of his office; the sacred cord wound round his waist, used to tie up prisoners, and the staff of office with its bunch of ribbons, stuck into his belt. The *topiri*, immured in an obsidian reserve, replied with eyes averted, and without changing his posture, to our questions. He mentioned briefly that a week or two previously a ceremony had taken place that it would have been interesting for us to see. A new *Tatouan* had been elected, and according to Huichol democratic procedure he had not been informed in advance of his candidature. As the office provides for no remuneration but imposes many onerous duties, he had been persuaded to accept nomination only after a short period of imprisonment without food. The *Tatouan* was now away on his rancho, recovering from the experience, and all his officers had gone off about their personal affairs. Somebody had had a premonitory dream, which had brought about a change in the date of the fiesta.

The shaman, always eager to promote our journalistic interests, asked the *topiri* if there were any prisoners in his charge at that moment, and was disappointed to hear that there were not. A pity, he said. The Huichols kept their malefactors in stocks. It would have made an attractive photograph.

A few more Huichols had drifted into view and we were doing our best to make friends, examining the details of their beautifully decorated clothing, when a distraction occurred. A *mestizo* carrying a rifle on his shoulder had appeared at the entrance to the village. He came towards us a short distance, walking with swinging hips, in a mincing effeminate way, and then stopped. There was a moment of absolute silence and some theatricality when, for a time, nothing moved; and then, without shifting the position of their bodies, the Huichols turned expressionless faces to the newcomer, who stood looking down from a slight rise in the maroon earth. It was a brooding Eisenstein composition of iron profiles and watching eyes set against deep shadows. Ravens were over us in the dark sky and the man with the gun looked from side to side, suddenly nervous, and began to kick in a desultory way at a horse's jawbone at his feet.

Two or three Huichols now moved towards him, casually and without evident purpose, and soon he was in the centre of a little group, which the shaman joined to begin a sharp questioning. The shaman asked him for his name, and he turned out to be none other than Adolfo Castañera – the associate of the man on the mule. He was asked now to give an exact account of his comings and goings, and this seemed to be unsatisfactory. Ramon asked him if any of the Huichols present would vouch for his respectability, and Adolfo pointed to a man whom he said had known him for several years, but the Huichol would only agree that he'd seen him once or twice. No more than that.

The word *malhechor*, used locally for bandit, came up, and Castañera was aggrieved, but still cool. Not only was he no outlaw himself, but he was one of their victims. As proof of this he took off his shirt to display the scars of a terrible wound in the stomach, produced by the exit of a dum-dum bullet, and we were invited to examine the tiny white circle in the skin of his back where the bullet had entered. He had been shot from ambush, he said, on 22 June 1969, on the trail we had just come down from Santa Clara, about five kilometres from San Andres. The argument that no man with such a wound could be other than innocent failed to impress the shaman. Adolfo was agreeable enough to allow David to photograph him, holding his rifle, and after that it was taken away from him. In a final attempt to establish a bond between himself and David and myself – the only other non-Indians present – he told us that he had visited San Diego, California, which is both the Paris and the El Dorado of Central America. He was a man of education, he said, and he had travelled the world. But the Huichol *topiri*, standing at his back, his sacred cord untied, knew nothing of this, and Castañera was led away in custody, while a messenger hurried from the village to find the reluctant *Tatouan* on his rancho and bring him back to preside over the 'court' proceedings.

Ramon had warned us that we must leave San Andres by four p.m. so as to be able to reach the mission by nightfall, and we were now impatient to see whatever there might be to see in the time that remained. However, the shaman was not to be found, and it seemed to me imprudent to take the law into our own hands and go off on our own. Societies such as these are governed by the most intricate protocol, and it is easy to give unwitting offence. I could never, for example, in the absence of the shaman, decide whether it was in order to photograph the village shrine, or to examine it too closely, or whether even we were being ill-mannered in sitting, as we did, on the long ceremonial bench outside the council house. I recalled the experience of a French friend who had ridden into a Moi village in the highlands of Vietnam and, tying his horse to the nearest post found that he had offered it – irrevocably – as a sacrifice to the ancestral spirits. In the circumstances a vigilant inactivity seemed called for, and we were relieved when Ramon eventually reappeared.

The news he brought accounted for his un-Indian state of agitation. He told us that he had just found the body of a murdered man in a house a few yards from were we sat. We followed him to it and went in just as the Huichols were lifting down the corpse from the space it had been crammed into, between the rafters and the roof. The shaman explained that he had sensed death in the village, and had been drawn by his instincts to this house, which was unoccupied and had been kept locked up for some months. He added the information, as if passing on facts that he had read in a newspaper, that the victim had been killed in the mountains and had been brought here to be hidden by a band of about six men. In this corner of the sierra, which abounded in ravines and caves, and where wild animals would soon have removed all traces of an abandoned corpse, it seemed strange to us that the assassins should bother to put themselves to such trouble. But who could say what motives – irrational though they might seem to us – were involved?

The dead man, identified as Miguel Garcia, had been killed by a gunshot wound in the right side of the chest, and the major cause for consternation in the village was that – according to the shaman's expert advice – he had died between two and three days before, and not only had putrefaction set in, but all the delicate machinery of the manipulation of the soul, which must begin its journey to the underworld five days after death, had been thrown completely out of gear by this delay.

Death had taken the village off its guard. At this moment we should all have gathered by the body to drink ritual beer, but there was none. There were no candles to be found either, no animal of any kind that could have decently been sacrificed, hardly enough maize flour even for the five funerary tortillas that would sustain the spirit on the first stage of its journey. What could be found of the dead man's possessions had been assembled for burial, but it was essential to include with them symbolic bodily parts: arms and legs, and a head, woven from some sacred material, that would replace the physical body as corruption advanced. None of this could be discovered, and the shaman had to make do with ordinary grass. The atmosphere was one of depressed improvization, against a background of the controlled sobbing of the dead man's sister.

The *Tatouan* and his officers now arrived, presenting stoic Indian faces to the ritual confusion. Wearing their ceremonial hats, decorated with buzzards' and eagles' feathers, they stalked in slow procession into the council house to begin their deliberations. A grave fifteen feet deep was almost finished outside the village's limits, but their first ruling was that, whatever the religious imperatives, the body must remain unburied until all the relatives had been assembled – and some of them lived on ranchos a day's ride away.

In this the shaman, who had called for immediate burial, was overruled. He was overruled too in the matter of the bandit suspect, who received a short and perfunctory trial and was released – seemingly for lack of sufficient evidence. The man was given back his gun, but as a concession to Ramon's objections it was unloaded and Ramon was allowed to take the bullets. He left the village, with a swagger emphasizing victory – and, departing, he shot us a last meaningful glance that was devoid of amity. In a way the verdict came as a relief. We were obliged now to accept the fact that in the sierra human life was cheap indeed. At first there had been hints of rough justice and, to the last, the shaman – still certain that the man would be found guilty – had insisted that we would take him back to Tepic with us, to hand him over to the federal police there. There now remained the uncomfortable possibility that somewhere in the forest between San Andres and Santa Clara an armed man with a grudge against the shaman might be lying in wait. In consequence, when we set off we walked well separated and in single file – the local method of reducing the risks inherent in such a situation.

Reaching the Nautla Gorge, we threw ourselves down to rest. The mission was only half an hour's scramble away down the mountainside and already the sun had fallen behind the peaks.

By this time our relationship with the shaman had grown close and cordial, and he chose this moment to create us honorary *compañeros* of the Huichol people, and formally invited us to set out with him on the annual peyote pilgrimage, which would start in twenty-five days' time. For the sixth time Ramon would lead his people, at the head of four captains, across mountain and desert for twenty days to Rial Catorce in the high desert of San Luis Potosí. We would march rapidly in single file, carrying nothing but bows, sacred tobacco, holy water and ritual implements, sustained on the journey by the virtue engendered by our own austerities.

Huichols regard peyote as deer that have transformed themselves by magic into the sacred cactus, so the peyote would not be simply collected, but 'hunted' with bows and arrows, and it would be prayed and sung to before being eaten. Afterwards, renewed by the visions we had imbibed, our faces painted with symbols of victory, we would set out again on the long march back to the Sierra Madre, in the knowledge that whatever our state of weakness and emaciation when we arrived, we would surely be rewarded by a long and good life.

It was an adventure of great attraction to both of us,

and Ramon agreed that if we found it impossible to make our arrangements at this short notice, the invitation could be renewed next year.

In the meantime there were aspects of the day's happenings that remained obscure, and as tactfully as I could, I asked Ramon if he could explain more clearly how, and at what point, he had decided that a dead body was hidden in the village, and, also, whether the *travesía* he had discovered on the trail from Santa Clara that morning had been in some way connected with this tragedy?

But here the blunt linguistic instrument of Castilian failed us both. The Huichols speak a version of Aztec, rich in nuance and undercurrents of allusion, that are untranslatable into the basic Spanish of a foreigner, and my categorical questions called for muted and conditional answers that could not be given. On one thing, however, he was definite. I had been unable to accept the story of a body being hidden by casual murderers in a village house. Did he really believe that the Huichol in San Andres had been killed by bandits?

'No,' he said. 'The man was killed because he wanted to be a shaman.'

We went on, thankful to arrive within sight of Santa Clara and its guardian dogs. The first owls were flying, a coyote snapped over the horizon, and a blue, mountain dusk had already fallen over the mission buildings when we arrived. The children had built their camp fires on the slopes, and when they saw us they came out to meet us, full of laughter and carrying their guitars.

1970

MEXICAN MOSAIC

'WHERE DO YOU carry your money?' asked the small middle-aged man at the back of the *rapido* bus from Mexicali, on the U.S. frontier, to Mazatlán.

He went on to suggest that I should keep a reasonable float of a few hundred pesos wherever I usually did and put the rest in my sock. His qualifications to advise on such precautionary measures were solidly based, for he was a long-distance bus driver by profession, travelling home as a passenger after a journey up to the border two days before, when his bus had been held up by bandits.

'But aren't they going to look in your shoes?'

'They're in too much of a hurry,' the bus driver said, 'and their nerves are shot to pieces. They grab whatever they can and they get out.'

Like so many law-abiding people dazzled by the charisma of violence, he seemed grateful for the experience and happy to find saving grace in the highwaymen who had carried rocks on to the lonely road and pointed a submachine-gun at his windscreen.

'They're not too bad,' he said. 'Say *buenos dias* to them, and they say *buenos dias* to you.' One of the passengers had mentioned that he was out of work and they'd given his money back, as well as being politeness itself to the women passengers.

There was always an adventure waiting round the corner on the long-distance buses, the driver said. It was a point of honour to get into a station on time and this sometimes meant pushing the cruising speed up to eighty miles an hour. On the last trip southwards he had hit a cow at full throttle and splashed it all over the bus, which had to be taken out of service and hosed down at the next town. It was a good thing, he said, to sit up at the back as he did, just as it was better when you flew anywhere to get as close as you could to the tail of the plane.

The bus driver was the first Mexican I spoke to on this journey, and like so many of his countrymen in subsequent random encounters, he immediately took charge of my welfare. The bus rampaged on through the long hot day, and then into a haggard nightscape of cactus and flint. The dreaming, hollow-eyed villages came and went, and lean men going home asleep on their horses awoke to kick them into desperate life and charge for the verge at the hideous outcry of our siren. We stopped at dreadful hours at woebegone staging points when passengers got down and staggered away carrying their fatigue like some three-dimensional burden as they went in search of food.

In these hallucinatory moments I foraged under the umbrella of my friend's protection. The dishes on offer at these places were strongly regional in character: pork cooked in chocolate, or tacos of meat in a maize-pancake sandwich. At one stopping point a man succeeded in selling a number of hydrogen-filled balloons to passengers who were too dazed to realize what they were buying. At another a cartomancer, crying, 'It isn't the betrayal so much as the doubt that kills', promised to tell males of the party whether or not their wives were being unfaithful in their absence. Occasionally there were pleasures on offer, other than the satisfaction of hunger, for those who were prepared to cram them into these few bleak moments in the dead of night. 'Travellers waited upon with speed and *formality*', said a notice displayed in one stark pull-in. But however speedy and formal the young ladies lurking rather hopelessly in the background might have been, the iron schedules of bus travel slammed the door on such adventures. 'Ten minutes,' the conductor had warned, 'and not a second more.' And in precisely ten minutes we were under way again.

At each major town faces changed as we lost fellow travellers who were by now old friends, and took on a fresh influx of strangers eager for membership of our temporary family. For a while we were on a sort of Canterbury pilgrimage by high-speed bus when eleven fat men from the Middle Ages got in, all of them called Francisco and all of them on their way to a prestigious shrine of the saint by that name. They rolled about the bus fizzing with excitement and forcing bottles of Montezuma beer on the other passengers, and when they settled, like true pilgrims, it was to tell stories endlessly. Their huge posteriors spread over a seat and a half wherever they sat, and a thin doctor, also a Francisco, who was travelling with them and hoped to get them all back alive, said: 'You may think these men are fat, but actually they're starving to death. All they ever eat is rice and beans. If you stuck a pin in them, they'd deflate.' It was twenty miles from the bus stop to the shrine, he said, and the intention was to walk the last seven miles barefoot. 'It could cut the soles of their feet about a bit,' the doctor said, 'but otherwise if they survive could do wonders for their general health.'

We dropped our pilgrims off in a mist-veiled morning full of cactus and circling buzzards a few miles before Tepic, and here we took on a Huichol Indian decked with feathers and beads and carrying a bow and a sheaf of arrows in a dry-cleaner's plastic cover. Eagles' pinions sprouted from the rim of his flat staw hat, and his tunic and pantaloons were densely embroidered with deer, pelicans and heraldic cats. He sat in noble isolation from the rest of us, moving only once to fill a paper cup with water from a tap at the back, then having rummaged for a while in his splendidly ornamented satchel, he found an Alka Seltzer, unwrapped it, dropped it into the water, and gulped down the result.

He got off at Tepic, capital of the Wild-Western, gun-slinging State of Nayarit, and I did, too, wanting to enquire after my old friend Ramon Medina, shaman of the Huichol people, with whom I had spent some time in the sierra exactly ten years before. The shaman was a unique artist, the originator of those extraordinary pictures in wool now seen in degenerate versions in Mexcian folk-art shops throughout the world. He was also Mexico's foremost bowman and a faith healer of such renown that he had been kept in Zapópan, the Lourdes of Mexico, for a year or two to treat the many sufferers from phobias and psychosomatic disorders attracted to that town. It had now become a matter of personal regret that I had fought shy of accepting his treatment for the affliction of a life-long nervous cough by allowing him to expectorate down my throat. I learned at Tepic, where the shaman's fame had been great, that he had died some years before, almost certainly murdered by one of the many gunmen that infest the sierra of Nayarit, and prey on the isolated Indian communities that have taken refuge there.

At this point in the journey I backslid. The original intention had been to travel by bus all the way from the U.S. border to the Guatemalan frontier with Mexico at Tapachula, but I had done 1,200 miles from the border and now, with a pair of lightweight trousers half worn through, and the earth shuddering like jelly every time I stepped down from the bus, there were still another 1,200 miles to go. The final straw was a failure to get a seat on three *rapidos* in succession, and I gave up and took the plane to Mexico City, to spend the night in the vast, unreal peace of the Maria Isabel-Sheraton Hotel. This was the only hotel in the downtown area of this turbulent city where a room was to be found. It is favoured by Americans and I mingled in its marble halls with Elks and Rotarians who had come there for conventions, faced up to its gargantuan meals, and listened to the soft, ubiquitous moan of its airport music.

The Sheraton's portions of food – this also applied to neighbouring restaurants – were so vast that they could not be contained on ordinary plates, and the pound or more of meat with all its garnishings was spread over an elongated metal dish. The vacuum-religiosity of such places was reflected on a card propped on the table which said, 'We owe it to "Him". Let us be big enough and grateful enough to acknowledge this fact today and each following day, and before partaking of this food, let each of us bow his head and give thanks.' The waiter said that about one third of the food he served was returned to the kitchen to go into the swill.

The hotel presents each guest with the Lloyd's (monthly) Economic Report, a complacent document which has nothing to offer the visitor but good cheer. A minimum increase in the private sector investment of 235 per cent was projected for the year. For the past year the nation showed a 7 per cent growth in real terms, and among the 152 member states of the United Nations it was in the 10 per cent having the highest living standards. A deal was afoot with the French to supply three nuclear power stations – and so on. From where one sat in the fairy palace of the Sheraton it was impossible to disbelieve that this was so. On the other hand, Mexico City, said by some to have a population numbering nearly 20 million and therefore to rank as the largest city in the world, is said by others to have the most extensive slums in the western hemisphere, which, when I spent some hours in them, showed little signs of improvement since the days of Dr Oscar Lewis's famous report. It has been said, too, that most Mexicans earn about £300 a year. Who is one to believe – Lloyd's, or the sociologists who deny that the vast revenues from oil and steel have any serious effect on the poverty of the man in the street?

Exercise was called for to cope with the digestion of the hotel's copious and indulgent meal, so I took a walk round the city block on which it is built, where I found seventeen indigent families camping out for the night in the street, these in most cases consisting of mother and two or three small children. They live there, and in the vicinity of the other luxury hotels, scraping a living as best they can, but for the most part dependent upon the charity of passers-by – in the main the travellers from overseas. Hard times are confronted cheerfully. One mother of three said, 'On the whole I can't complain. We come to places like this because foreigners are more generous than our own people. My husband is a labourer back in our village but he's always out of work, and I usually do better than he does. To tell you the truth the children enjoy an outing to the city. It's a change for them. Anyone can put up with sleeping on a clean pavement, and if it rains we can always go to the arcades. If any of the children come out in sores or pick up a cough you often find that someone who happens to be a doctor will stop and give you something for it, so in this way it's even better than being at home.'

Extreme poverty, as I have always observed in Mexico, is in no way inconsistent with happiness.

There was a choice of routes from Mexico City to the deep south, and someone recommended an east-coast approach through the swamps and the oilfields of the State of Tobasco, so I flew to Villahermosa and there hired a self-drive car, so as to be able to reach areas not served by the buses. In this simple operation an unexpected complication arose. Villahermosa, an oil-rich city, glutted with cars, and on the edge of an area currently producing the staggering total of 2 million barrels of oil a day, was a place where it was as hard to buy petrol as it is to find freshly caught fish in an English seaside town. The manager of the car-hire firm presided over a row of shining new Mexican-made Volkswagen Beetles, but all of them had empty tanks, and a pint of petrol had to be syphoned with enormous difficulty from his own car to get me to the one filling station, where by luck and by favour I managed to fill her up at 30p per gallon.

Villahermosa draws a few tourists by reason of being within easy reach of the Mayan pyramids of Palenque. It offers striking contrasts. The sudden raucous prosperity engendered by oil is grafted on a rootstock of impassive Mexican calm. One sees a heron prospecting an abandoned tanker for edible ticks in the belief that it has come upon some gigantic new species of zebu cattle, while a bird of the same order occasionally mucks in with the guests in the swimming pool of the local hotel. This establishment has both character and charm. Beautiful Mayan waitresses serve the mettlesome *plat du jour* – which may be tripe cooked in chillies – with the dignity of priestesses officiating at a religious ceremony. Frogs like miniature race horses gallop up and down the air-conditioned passages, and in the evening guests are entertained with 'Rose Marie' and 'Pale Hands I Loved' on the Yamaha organ.

The audience, largely Japanese on package-deal tours, are mystified by the music but eager to show appreciation, and clap whenever they can. In the morning they are up betimes, cameras loaded and the wide-brimmed Mexican sombreros imported nowadays from Korea strapped to their luggage, ready for the jungle-smothered ruins. The hallmark of an advanced society is obsession with plumbing, so the Japanese lady in control of the group presents herself at the reception, bowing and smiling, to make a routine complaint about non-functioning flushes, after which the party is on its way.

Sixty per cent of the State of Tobasco, of which Villahermosa is the capital, is swampland. It rains here softly and remorselessly for ten months on end, and as it rains the waters rise gently and spread their lily-decked margins over more and more of the landscape. When the sun finally shines it is on a scene that is deceptively meek. Aquatic plants, many of them sporting magnificent blooms, quilt the spread water to suggest a fictitious solidity, but only Indians can live here, and about 60,000 of them actually do.

The thing to see near Villahermosa is the invention born of desperation and ingenuity by which the survivors of the redoubtable Chontal race, chased into the marsh by their Spanish conquerors, managed to stay alive. Using their bare hands they scooped slime from the bottom of the swamp and piled it up to form mounds and ridges above the water level, and on these they planted their beans and their squash.

A few years ago government agriculturists appeared to have noticed what was going on – and had been for centuries – and decided that all that was required was the application of scientific farming methods to develop the *camellón* system, as it is called, into an important new source of food.

Teams of experts arrived with the fertilizers, the insecticides, the new types of seeds and plants, and, above all, the giant dredgers borrowed from PEMEX, the state oil concern, with which the great swamp was to be dominated and encouraged to produce the new vegetable abundance. The dredger would build the *camellones* at a hundred times the speed of men working without tools, and the hollows left where the mud had been gouged from the swamp's bed would be stocked with suitable fish. A trial batch of 600 approved families were to be presented with this living space created from virtually nothing and, working under scientific supervision, were to produce the new wealth. Exactly three years had passed since the beginnings of this hopeful experiment when I drove out to visit Nacajuca, headquarters of the project, a few miles down the road from Villahermosa, to see how things had gone.

The rain, having fallen for some forty weeks on end, had stopped only a few days before, and the tropical sun had begun the slow process of sucking away the water. Most of the Chontals were out of sight, busy as usual with survival, but a few privileged ones who had managed to establish a foothold by the side of the raised metalled road carried on their normal occupations, knee-deep in water, mending and making things, cooking, washing the clothes and child-minding with an indifference that suggested they had forgotten the flood's existence. A man busied himself with wire to mark out the boundaries of a garden two feet under water. A funeral party, all its members properly drunk, staggered and splashed towards a hillock where the coffin they carried would be temporarily interred to await reburial in the cemetery when it dried out. The most extraordinary vision was that of cattle swimming to feed on floating beds of water-hyacinths, only heads and shoulders showing above the water, the lavender blossom trailing from their lips.

It was about midday when we reached the spot where they were building up new *camellones*. The dredger plunged its huge claw into the swamp, scooping up a ton of marsh at a time to drop it on the half-completed bank. A lorry dumped a load of cocoa bean husks on the mud and rotting vegetation as a small army of Chontals moving like sleep-walkers arrived with their mattocks to nudge the husks into the unsatisfactory soil.

The Chontals inherit elaborate social graces from noble forebears, and they are saturated with the sly, defensive humour of the underdog. When I asked the man in charge of this party what the goings-on on his Tarzan T-shirt were all about, he displayed the ruin of his teeth in a stealthy grin and said, 'These are the legends of a primitive people.' I understood that I was included in this category. When these men sat down to their midday meal it was clear that they were eating the same old vitamin-deficient maize cakes and beans that the Indian Institute had described in its book on the project as not only inadequate for the needs of the body but detrimental to the mental faculties.

Later, the director of the project spoke of his experiences with good-humoured resignation. He had learned a lot from the men he had set out to teach, he said. Probably as much as they had learned from him. Some of their attitudes had shocked and surprised him a little at first. He had run up against the hard fact that they had no sense of money or trade and this being so the marketable surpluses the Institute had hoped for with which they might have bought such consumer goods as transistor radios, or even Japanese mopeds, were out. 'I accept now,' he said, 'that the Chontal wants to work with his family, produce just enough to live on and consume all he produces.'

He had been stunned by such things as their tolerance in the matter of the irresponsible idleness of certain of their fellow workers. The idea was that ten men should form their own little co-operative nucleus to farm a *camellón* efficiently, but it didn't work out that way.

'You find two or three don't want to work at all. They just sit round all day and talk about their dreams, and the others don't mind in the slightest. You and I would resent a situation like that, but they don't. They never criticize each other and you'll never believe how conservative they are. We introduced new vegetables, but most of them were attacked by plant diseases, and when we got them to use sprays they poisoned the fish. We found out that the cocoa bean husks they've always used seem to be the only fertilizer that works on that soil.

'Their diet's terribly short of protein, so we persuaded them to raise pigs, but when the time came they wouldn't kill them. "Christ," they say, "I can't kill that animal. I love him like my brother. Kill him after I've been giving him a wash and brush-up, and food out of my own mouth every day for the last six months? Excuse me, your honour, but what do you take me for – a cannibal?" '

Scarlet dragonflies flew in through the office window, and the director cuffed them away, and laughed. 'After all, what are we after? Our hope and intention was to fill their stomachs, because everything depends on that. Do you know what we've discovered in the end? We've learned that the traditional agriculture of these people's ancestors fills their stomachs faster than we can. So technicians are out. Insecticides are out. Diversification is out. We sow by the moon and the rain, and we sow maize, beans, squash, yuccas and plantains. We've gone right back to the Mayan solution of the pre-conquest. All they needed was a little land to be able to take off. At least we've given them that.'

The only road due south from Villahermosa crosses the high sierra, and no driver should take it on in a car which cannot be repaired by the blacksmith–electrician team likely to be found in any of the small towns passed in a day's driving. There are terrific gradients, and many bends, some spread with the mud of recent landslides. The forest that climbs through up to the cool, thin air displays tropical embellishments: parrots surfacing suddenly like a shoal of glittering fish from the quilted foliage, an occasional toucan, a scrambling, raccoon-like animal in the road. A café has been built at the highest point, with wolves' and bears' skins tacked to its walls, where the boss entertains the occasional customer after serving the food with the extraordinary knack he has developed of catching the flies that have settled on his plate – eight to ten in a single swipe of the paw.

It was shortly after enjoying this experience that I stopped for two Americans stranded by trouble with the automatic transmission in their opulent new car. There were thirty miles of wary driving round the edge of a number of precipices between them and the last town they had passed, and I had to break the news to them that the situation that faced them was roughly the same. I offered them a lift, but they wanted to stay with the car, so, promising to try to arrange a rescue, I drove on.

The next town was a mile or two off the main road and, stopping at a cantina to enquire the way, I found myself talking to the local chief of police, who had just arrested two youths for making an affray and had paused for a beer before taking his prisoners back. I told him about the stranded car, and he offered to help me find a mechanic. He led the way down to the town, and courteously invited me into the jail where the two prisoners were put in one of a row of cage-like cells of the type shown in Western movies, where they continued their arguments and threats. We then set off in the almost hopeless search for someone with an experience of automatic transmissions.

This town was a museum-piece of the traditional Mexican scene: a square with a seething market, a general store stacked with cartridges, nails and tattered stockfish, a pub called 'I'll be here when you get back', a main street with trenches hacked out of its surface to slow down the traffic and a great number of people going nowhere in particular, including a man with a pig on a lead, and another carrying a canary in a cage. For all the world it was a multi-coloured Mexican version of a Lowry. Inevitably fireworks lit surreptitiously popped here and there, hissing thirty feet into the air to explode with a blue cauliflower of smoke. The mechanic's wife, when in the end we tracked him down, said that he was asleep, but the chief of police would have none of this and led the way through the house into a backyard where we found him soldering together a toy spacecraft that had to be ready for some child's saint's day. In the end he agreed to go up the road and see what could be done. Had he any experience of automatic transmissions? the police chief asked. No, the man told him, but he had his intuitions. 'Tell them to flog the thing and try a Volkswagen next time they come to this country,' the chief of police said.

San Cristobal de las Casas is the last town of stature of the Deep South before reaching the Guatemalan frontier. It is built in the high mountains, an enclave of the colonial past, its walls pitted with the cannonballs of forgotten revolutions, and its streets full of sharp, Alpine colour under a sweetly discordant muddle of old bells. The misfortune of San Cristobal is that the Pan-American Highway runs through its outskirts, and down it has come the advance guard of the invasion of our times, including 2,000 American hippies who have settled in the town and attempted, with signal lack of success, to copy the appearance and life-style of the Indians who form the great majority of the surrounding population.

The presence of these expatriates has stimulated a never deeply buried anti-American feeling – based supposedly in the memory of ancient oppressions and interventions – and insulting graffiti are frequently scrawled on the walls of the houses in which they lodge. Although many young Americans have tried to transform themselves into Indians, so far only one Indian is known to have returned the compliment by becoming a pseudo-hippy, having abandoned the industrious, hyperactive life of his people to spend much of his time in one of the cafés, imitating a hippy imitating an Indian.

The State of Chiapas, of which San Cristobal was the old capital, is on the last frontier of tourism in Mexico; a frontier now widely breached, and in course of demolition. Mayan tribes who survived the holocaust of the Spanish conquest, and contrived to keep a nucleus of the old civilization intact, find themselves faced by a more ruthless destroyer of their culture as the tourists pour in.

In the past half-century, the anti-clericalism of Mexican revolutionary governments, plus in this case geographical isolation, has favoured the re-emergence of the Indian personality, and even in the end the un-concealed practice of the ancestral religion. In some churches the Catholic priest has been replaced by the Indian shaman. This return to the ancestral customs and beliefs has sometimes gone along with a rejection of valuable and positive aspects of the dominant civilization. Peasants have preferred to bundle all their goods on their backs to bring them to market rather than use a wheeled vehicle, and in Amatenango, a village devoted to the making of pottery near San Cristobal, a well-meaning attempt by an American woman to convert the villagers to the use of the potter's wheel led to her murder.

The violence of our times has spread in all directions down the Mexican roads. San Cristobal has been transformed in a single decade from a town of extraordinary tranquillity into one in which it is no longer safe to walk in the streets after dark. Both Indians and whites have been frequently attacked and occasionally murdered, and women of both races have been raped. The tribal elders watch what seems to them the decay of the Western world and struggle to prevent the spread of its contagion into the Indian areas.

Indians feel themselves more threatened by metaphysical than physical violence. In the recent past they have been largely left to live their lives in peace in their own way, but the mountain villages are now under assault by groups of tourists who offend by their permissiveness, often behaving insultingly – sometimes, as the Indians see it, in a sacrilegious manner, when they force their way into their shrines and sacred places. These invasions provoke violent reactions. Tourists have been frequently attacked in villages such as Chamula, which attracts great crowds of foreigners on feast days and is now patrolled by cudgel-armed vigilantes determined to keep the invaders in their place.

I drove up to Chamula with an Indian friend without

whose help it would have been impossible to break out of the quarantine imposed upon visitors from the outside world. It was a Sunday morning, and the wooden shacks round the fine colonial church – now taken over for the performance of Indian ceremonies – were afloat in a freezing mist. A coachload of tourists from a local agency had already arrived, and they were fiddling uneasily with their cameras which could only be used surreptitiously, and with some risk to themselves under the mistrustful eyes of the Indians with their staves. In the last week a stern notice had been put up, and an English translation supplied:

ALL VISITORS. IT IS STRICTLY FORBIDDEN TO TAKE ANY PHOTOGRAPHS IN THIS MUNICIPIO AND OF THESE FESTIVITIES CARNIVAL SO THAT OUR CUSTOMS AND RELIGIOUS TRADITIONS WILL BE RESPECTED.
SINCERELY

NOTE. INFRINGEMENT WILL BE SEVERELY PUNISHED.

The Chamulas set out to show that they meant what they said. A set-pattern exchange of compliments and courtesies had to be gone through with half a dozen dignitaries of varying ranks, and bitter coffee drunk with the *Alcalde*, dressed like a minor Spanish nobleman of the sixteenth century, before we could be given the freedom of the village!

Even then two *mayores* carrying cudgels slung like rifles from their shoulders were assigned to keep an eye on us. Their first act was to conduct us to the lock-up where two prisoners were held under austere conditions, to make it clear what happened in Chamula to people who broke the rules. We were told that these two men were being held, until they showed sincere repentance, 'for failing to comply with their civic duties'. The climate of the mountain villages is authoritarian, with a reverence for hard work, and tasks for all, men, women and children alike, are allotted according to age, sex, and ability. Idleness is more than frowned upon.

The visit to the church that followed was the most remarkable experience, in its way, of the whole Mexican journey. Many tourists had had their cameras smashed trying to photograph these scenes where Indians worshipped in the old style, crouched on the bare pavement among the twinkle of innumerable candles and the red and white blossoms spread to represent the souls of the living and the dead, the theatrical presence of the shamans escorted by their guitarists, the incantations, the frenzy of possession and the ritual drunkenness. Two rows of Christian saints, twenty or more of them, carved larger than life, blood-striped and formidable in their anguish and wrath, looked down on this scene. Hanging from their necks were the original mirrors given by the Conquistadors to the tribal ancestors in exchange for their gold, and they seemed to be held here like captives or hostages in this wholly non-Christian scene. Realizing that the memory could not cope with the bizarre richness of the surroundings, I took out a notebook, but one of our guardians, ever watchful, signed to me to put it away. Even note-taking was prohibited in this Mayan holy of holies.

Indians have been attracted to settle in the Chamula

region for two reasons, the first a spiritual, and the second a highly practical one. A few miles away, behind Tzinakantán, rises up the highest peak in the State of Chiapas, and this is regarded as a rich repository of animal souls, the Naguals, with which the Mayas of this area link their own. Anthropologists are in dispute about the precise nature of this empathy, or soul-making, and my Chamula friend was bewildered at what he saw as the imaginative poverty of Western intellectuals who were unable to grasp the basic simplicities of Indian metaphysical thought. He explained that most of his people, although not all, developed a mystic affinity with one or several animals of the 'noble' kind, for example, the jaguar and the deer, and that the human benefited from the instincts and the sensitivities of the animal, although since his well-being ran a parallel course with that of his Nagual, he was bound to suffer from its death.

The village of Tzinakantán being in such close proximity to the magic mountain, it followed that this was the best possible place for an Indian to spend all the time in he could. When we drove over from Chamula we found about a thousand of them, dressed in all their finery, clustered on the terraces in its centre to discuss their problems, or getting drunk in the well-conducted, ritual fashion that fosters visions and dreams. The practical attraction of the region lies in deposits of fine clay used in the making of pottery. A number of villages have exploited this since the remotest times, and in pre-Hispanic days their production was exported to all parts of the Mayan empire. Most celebrated of the potters' villages is Amatenango, where the potter's wheel was once rejected in so emphatic a fashion.

Amatenango's tragedy is also the vicinity of the Pan-American Highway, passing within half a mile of the low hill on which it is built. The life of this village as described by a traveller in the 1950s followed archaic ceremonial patterns, most of which have been brusquely swept away. It was the habit – still observed in other less accessible villages – for the male head of the household to rise in the small hours to perform the principal act of creation, that of lighting the fire, after which the family gathered for a three-hour exchange of ideas and discussion of moral problems before the day's work began. Thereafter the men occupied themselves with such manual tasks as digging and preparing the clay, while creative activity passed into the hands of the women, who fashioned the pots, shaping them with their hands, smoothing surfaces with the instruments employed by their ancestors for at least 1,000 years, and painting them with traditional abstract designs. At this point the men would be called in to make fire again, and the pots would be baked – as now – in bonfires of brushwood lit in the village streets.

Every stage in the pot's preparation required its small ceremonial act, its mumbled invocation, or its libation, and when finished it was regarded with pride, and with respect for the impulse of creation translated to the clay. A potter would be happy, as she might in the case of the surplus puppy, to find it a good home. The medieval craftsman's desire to impose his personality upon his production survived, as it still does in the remoter textile village of Bochil, where an order for a large number of the exquisite embroidered blouses which are its speciality was recently turned down because the buyer insisted

on absolute uniformity, whereas by tradition no two
garments could ever be exactly the same.

Amatenango was the last of the villages we visited, and
it was immediately clear that something was wrong. It is
a picturesque place with well-made wooden huts
screened by high cane fences. The women's blouses,
brilliantly embroidered in reds and yellows in imitation
of tropical birds, remain as yet unchanged – although
they are certain to go – and the spectacle of these
magnificent creatures at work firing their pots in the
street bonfires is irresistible to the camera of any tourist.
The village has indeed been featured in the promotional
literature of several tour operators, bringing in the main
visitors from Japan and from France. At the moment of
our arrival a Club Méditerranée group was just about to
leave and was being besieged by a horde of the only ill-
mannered Indian children I have ever encountered,
selling ugly pottery toys, demanding to be photographed for payment, and when refused shouting insults
in broken French.

My Chamula friend led the way to the house of a
potter he knew, where the feeling of disharmony became
stronger. There were no words in the Tzotzil language
spoken in the villages for the processes of trade, for
stock, profits, discounts, competition, turnover, etc., so
the villagers who find themselves drawn into commerce
are obliged to turn to Spanish, and these people were
speaking Spanish most of the time.

The complex protocol of village life had been largely
abolished. On the occasion of this visit we should have
been courteously seated, but thereafter kept waiting in
near silence outside the house while the Lares and the
Penates of the home accustomed themselves to our

presence before being invited to enter. But what was the point of such a procedure when almost daily groups of excited tourists would arrive to stand and stare, to point their cameras, and even to push their way into the houses without further ceremony?

People had too much time on their hands, too, and almost certainly too much money. Men were mooching about the streets, hands in pockets, dazed with their indigestible leisure. There was a village shop with canned beer on sale, and where the rude little girls, whose mothers could now afford to dress them in drab factory-made dresses, bought ice-cream with the money extorted from tourists.

The woman of the house explained that it used to take her family four days of common endeavour to make a pot of the largest size, for which she was paid about £3, but that by arrangement with the couriers who brought the parties of tourists she now charged the equivalent of £2 to allow herself to be photographed making a pot. The suspicion grew that the pots were no longer made for sale. It was a suspicion strengthened by the plastic buckets stocked by the village store and a depressing feature of local markets.

What the village still makes and sells is pottery toys, although these are no longer of the artistic calibre of those once made here and offered in fairs all over South Mexico. In the old days they were models of jungle animals, of alligators, armadillos, anteaters and the great cats, and the Indians' insight, their special comprehension of the animal world, had enabled them, sometimes in the very grotesqueness of these objects, to capture something of the quintessential quality of their living models.

These works of art have now vanished, and are to be found only in collections or museums. The new kind of buyers brought here in the air-conditioned coaches remained unimpressed by Indian art, although they were on the lookout for colourful souvenirs of their travels. The weavers of Bochil refused to admit Donald Duck into their traditional designs, but the potters of Amatenango surrendered. One of the tourist couriers gave them a sample of the cuddlesome toy he believed no tourist could resist, and he was right – Amatenango now turns out large numbers of Disney-style pottery kangaroos, and, sad to say, so far has taste been corrupted that Indians even buy these for their own children.

Now is the time to see South Mexico. Nothing can dim the glory of the great pre-Hispanic ruins and the great colonial towns, but outside that, in ten years it will be all Amatenango.

1980

MANHUNT

IN 1972, Dr Mark Münzel, an anthropologist working in Paraguay, reported wholesale enslavement, torture and massacre of the Guayaki Indians, among whom he was conducting his field studies. The Guayaki, who once occupied the whole of the forests of eastern Paraguay, have in recent years been reduced to a few bands roaming an area as large, perhaps, as Wales. They are of unique ethnic interest in that in a high proportion of cases they possess fair skin – for which reason they are sometimes known as 'white Indians'. They live as hunters and gatherers, and are notable poets, composers of epics and laments of extraordinary beauty.

Like all the forest Indians of South America the Guayaki have always suffered the persecution of settlers, ranchers and agriculturists, but until recent years they have been able to survive by withdrawing further and further into the depths of the forest. With the forest's gradual destruction and its replacement by ranching and farmland, their position has become increasingly desperate, and their hunger greater. These lovers of nature in all its forms – who actually embrace and talk to trees – are non-aggressive, and there is no recorded instance of a Guayaki having drawn his bow against a settler without provocation, but here and there hunger, through the removal of game, has caused them to kill a cow, with instant and terrible reprisals. In 1972, then, it seemed that official policy called for their elimination, or 'sedenterization' by forcible removal from the forest into a small reserve; the Colonia Nacionál Guayaki.

This operation was attended by atrocious circumstances. Professional Indian-killers were employed to carry out the raids into the forest. In many cases adult Indians were simply shot on sight, and the fate of their children was to be sold as slaves to farmers all over eastern Paraguay – a fact which has been confirmed by the accounts of numerous travellers in the area. Reports reached the international press, including that of this country, that so great was the glut of child slaves that their market price had fallen as low as five dollars. Later the figure fell to $1.50. At this time Dr Münzel and his wife happened to be working on the collection and translation of Guayaki poems in the neighbourhood of Cecilio Baez, where the reservation had been established, and he was already familiar with Jesús Pereira, the camp's administrator, an ageing manhunter with a criminal record, now transformed into a government official. Pereira still drew his gun on slight provocation, and his method of disciplining recalcitrant Guayakis at the camp was to cram them into a wooden frame called the 'tronco', in which the victim, unable to sit down or stand up, was left as long as necessary in full sun. He was a notorious sexual pervert, attracted to very young girls. Münzel was at the camp on one occasion when a batch of captured Indians was brought in, and he says that Pereira offered him an immature girl of about eleven, presumably to keep him quiet.

Thereafter, Dr Münzel visited the camp on several occasions. He noticed extraordinary variations in the number of its inhabitants. Although Indians were constantly being brought in, the number present on the reservation never exceeded 200. By the end of July 1972 there were sixty fresh graves to be counted, and Münzel calculated that seventy-five Guayakis had disappeared since March of that year. He also recorded a great disparity in the sexes of the captives. There were hardly any girls between the age of five and puberty. Female slaves in this age-group attracted the best prices on the market, and Münzel was forced to assume that a clandestine trade in slaves was being carried on. All the evidence – not only that of Münzel but of Paraguayan intellectuals and leaders of the Paraguayan Church who have publicized the facts of the Colonia Nacionál Guayaki – leads to the view that this was a camp through which the remaining Indian population of eastern Paraguay was doomed to pass into servitude or oblivion.

For obvious reasons Münzel's visits to the camp soon came to an end, after which a curtain of secrecy descended on its operations. For all this the manhunters seem to have felt no shame if by some accident the general public happened to witness them at their work – nor in fact did the general public evince any signs of the moral outrage one would have expected. 'I was on the bus to Asunción, when it made the usual stop at Arroyo Guasú. We heard that *señuelos* had just brought in a large number of Guayakis, and all the passengers got down to see them.' They found the Guayakis, guarded by the *señuelos*, bathing naked in the river. A passing car stopped. 'A woman and her two daughters got down.

One of them went down to the river's bank and took a child feeding at the breast from its mother, and went with it back to the car. The woman made no attempt to stop her or even cry out. She seemed petrified.' The writer of this account, a Paraguayan zoologist, Dr Luigi Miraglia, rushed after the abductress and took the child back. One wonders how many more such pathetic human souvenirs were taken when the hunters came in with their prey on that, and so many other days.

The term *señuelo* calls for explanation. *Señuelos* are 'tame' Guayakis turned hunter. Wild Guayakis cannot be taken by a white man in what, to him, is an impenetrable forest, but they can easily be captured by their own kind, armed with the belief shared by Indians of both conditions that the whites are jaguars in human form, and that when a Guayaki is captured by a jaguar, he too becomes a jaguar and is compelled to capture more of his own people. When the free Guayakis find themselves face to face with the 'jaguars' they throw down their bows, offer no resistance, make no attempt to escape. With their capture, they lose their humanity. The magic power of their chiefs is lost; the ceremonies are forgotten, the musical instruments thrown aside. Their only purpose in life now is to hunt as jaguars themselves. The *señuelo*'s immediate reward is the wives of the free men he captures.

In the summer of 1972 the Roman Catholic Church of Paraguay stated its grave concern over these events, and announced that it had informed the Holy See, while the Paraguayan anthropologists – Father Bartolomé Meliá, and Professor Chase Sardi – and the zoologist Dr Luigi Miraglia made a public declaration of genocide. In the resulting scandal Jesús Pereira was relieved of his functions and served a short term in prison. The administration of the sinister Colonia Nacionál Guayaki was then transferred to Mr Jack (Santiago) Stolz, of the New Tribes Mission – a North American Protestant missionary sect which combines a streamlined business approach with religious fundamentalism in dealing with problems of conversion. The mission has its own air service and radio transmitters, and three of its four centres in Paraguay are provided with airstrips.

A few months after Mr Stolz's takeover there were reported to be only twenty Indians left on the reservation. However in February 1973 a German army officer, who succeeded in visiting the camp in the guise of a tourist, found a group of fifteen or twenty 'obviously just arrived, in a desperate state of mind, just sitting around passively and staring at the ground'. A North American working on the reservation told him that these had just been brought in by none other than the old convicted manhunter, Jesús Pereira, who had caught a whole band and afterwards divided up the captives, some for the reservation, some for sale, and some for a farm he was now running with slave labour. The Jesuit Father Meliá writing in June 1973 to the German firm Farbwerke Hoechst, one of the original sponsors of the reservation, said that in the first nine months of the Stolz incumbency some 120 Guayakis had disappeared. It had been established that on 2 April 1973 more Indians had been brought into the reservation from the Itakyry region, but at this time no visits were allowed and therefore no investigations possible. At this time, Mark Münzel says in a report published by the International Work Group for Indigenous Affairs (Denmark), 'there

[were] signs that hunger was a problem on the reservation after the "arrival" of new Indians'. A letter from a Paraguayan contact said, 'There was a Guayaki who, in order to be able to buy something to eat, sold his son to some settlers for 80 guaranies [25p].'

Hunger is also mentioned in a letter written on 1 May 1973 by the Paraguayan rancher Mr Arnaldo Kant to Mr Nelido Rios, at that time assistant to the administrator of the reservation.

> Yesterday Mr Jack (Santiago) Stolz, administrator of the Colonia Guayaki was here ... He threatened to report me because I had that group of Guayakis you had gathered for me. I explained to him that I had them on your request, and only to prevent them from being used as slaves ... I was struck by the fear that this man [Jack Stolz] inspires in these Indians: when they noticed he was there [to return them to the reservation], they started to run away into the forest. The women wept, telling me they did not want to return to the camp because there they were given no food ... The administrator claimed payment for the work the Guayakis had done cleaning up around their houses, and I gave him the sum of 2,500 Gs., as proved by the enclosed receipt ...

The receipt, given at Cecilio Baez on 30 April 1973, is 'for labour performed by a group of Guayakis'. According to Mr Stolz, he wanted the money only in order to pay it to the Indians later on.

It should be understood that by this time the forest sheltering the Guayaki had been cleared to leave the reservation surrounded to a great depth by ranches and farms, and that no Indians had been seen anywhere in the vicinity since the great manhunts of 1972. In the unlikely event of any Guayaki leaving the forest to enter the reservation of his own free will, he would have had to travel for many miles across these cleared areas, now the property of settlers said to be prepared to shoot Indians on sight. Despite this the population at Cecilio Baez showed a sudden increase, reaching 110 by June 1973. At this time, Mark Münzel, back in Frankfurt, received a letter from a local contact to say that: 'The New Tribes missionaries are now hunting by motor vehicles for Guayakis in the region of Igatimi (100 miles from Cecilio Baez) in order to reintegrate them into the reservation.' Nevertheless, a visitor to the reservation on 23 August 1973 counted only twenty-five Indians – who were considerably outnumbered by the missionaries and their families. There was an upswing in population again by 17 September when (by Münzel's account), 'according to the North American missionary ... a band of forty-five Guayakis were brought to the reservation on a truck, "by the decision of God" and with the help of the Native Affairs Department of the Ministry of Defence, and of local police authorities from the region of Laurel, Department of Alto Paraná'. Thus, by the end of September, there should have been some seventy Indians on the reservation, but in January 1974, when it was visited by *New York Times* correspondent Jonathan Kandell, less than fifty were counted. The reservation continued to devour Indians.

In March 1974 the International League for the Rights of Man, joined by the Inter-American Association for Democracy and Freedom, charged the Government of

Paraguay with complicity in the enslavement and geno-
cide of the Guayaki Indians in violation of the United
Nations' Charter, the Genocide Convention and the
Universal Declaration of Human Rights.

In a protest to the United Nations' Secretary-General,
documented by four annexes, eye-witness accounts and
photographs, the organizations stipulated the following
violations leading to 'the wholesale disappearance of a
group of human beings', the Guayaki ethnic group:
(1) enslavement, torture and killing of the Guayaki
Indians in reservations in eastern Paraguay; (2) with-
holding of food and medicine from them resulting in their
deaths by starvation and disease; (3) massacre of their
members outside the reservations by hunters and
slave traders with the toleration and even encouragement
of members of the government and with the aid of the
armed forces; (4) splitting up of families and selling
into slavery of children, in particular girls for prostitution; and (5) denial and destruction of Guayaki
cultural traditions, including use of their language,
traditional music and religious practices.

On 8 March, Senator Abourezk, supported by forty-
four other senators, took the U.S. Senate floor 'to
denounce genocidal activities still rampant in Paraguay'.
Revealing that he had a copy of a receipt for work done
by slaves from the Colonia Nacionál Guayaki, he went
on: 'While on the reservation the Indian slaves are
discouraged from using their own language, and music is
expressly forbidden. The death rate from diseases of
malnutrition and sheer lack of will to survive is one of
the highest in the world.' The senator called for the
cutting-off of aid to Paraguay. He concluded: 'A
government which is bent on the mass extermination of

part of its people does not deserve our aid any more than a convicted and professed killer deserves a welfare check.'

Following Senator Abourezk's speech, the U.S. Ambassador to Paraguay was recalled and the senator and his supporters were privately admonished by the ambassador, who reminded them that the abiding friendship of Paraguay was indispensable in the framework of American hemispheric defence. The U.S. press remained strangely unresponsive to the news from Paraguay. Professor Richard Arens, Counsel to the League for the Rights of Man, says of this episode: 'A careful survey of the national media ... left us solely with an impression of a consciously or unconsciously determined news blackout.'

Repercussions in Paraguay were rapid. On 28 April 1974, the Department of Missions of the Paraguayan Episcopal Conference sent a letter to the Asunción daily newspaper *La Tribuna*, containing the following passage: 'Our secretariat has in its possession documentation of cases of massacre, cases which, moreover, have been partly published in your very paper.' The letter was signed by the Bishop of the Chaco region, Mgr Alejo Ovelar, and by Father Bartolomé Meliá, respectively president and secretary of the organization.

A second letter to *La Tribuna*, on 8 May 1974, said:

The Department of Missions of the Paraguayan Episcopal Conference has denounced and denounces, basing its denunciations on concrete data which has been duly investigated, the existence of cases of genocide ... [It] desires there be a sweeping investigation, especially into the situation of certain indigenous groups of Paraguay, who are especially threatened in their ethnic survival . . .

Next day the Paraguayan Minister of Defence, General Marcial Samaniego, called a conference to discuss these allegations. The minister did not attempt to deny that crimes against the Indians had taken place. He stressed however that there was no *intention* of destroying the Guayaki, and thus, by definition, genocide was excluded. 'Although there are victims and victimizer, there is not the third element necessary to establish the crime of genocide – that is "intent". Therefore, as there is no "intent", one cannot speak of "genocide".' (Asunción, *ABC Color*, 9 May 1974.)

Thereafter whatever news breached the silence had been discouraging. Latest reports from Paraguay suggested that the New Tribes missionaries pursued their aims with undiminished zeal, and Mr Jack Stolz continued to 'attract' Indians – as the euphemism puts it – with methods only too similar to those employed by his predecessor Mr Jesús Pereira. Pereira was still around, too, the master now of some fifty slaves, and engaged in continual incursions into the forest on his own account. A new Guayaki group had been located in Amambay, in the far north-east, and an expedition planned against it. Colonel Infanzón, Director of the Native Affairs Department, responsible in its time for the administrations both of Mr Pereira and Mr Stolz, had said: 'In spite of all our critics, we shall go on fighting and working, because we do not wish to leave unfinished the work we have started.'

In October 1974, Donald McCullin and I went to

Paraguay for the *Sunday Times* Magazine to try to find out what was happening.

The opinion of a contact in Asunción was that we should not make formal application to the Paraguayan Ministry of Defence to visit Cecilio Baez, because permission might well be denied, and even if granted, we should be sacrificing the element of surprise. Professor Chase Sardi, who had accompanied the correspondent of the *New York Times* in January, described their mission as a waste of time, because of advance notice given to the camp's administration, who were suitably prepared. Donald and I discussed the advice but felt obliged to reject it, because there was no certainty that having mounted an expedition to reach Cecilio Baez – in a country in which we supposed that every move made by a foreigner is under observation – we should be admitted to the reservation. It was conceivable, moreover, that any such abortive effort might be followed by expulsion from the country.

We therefore made application for the visit, and were duly summoned into the presence of Colonel T. Infanzón. It was hard to believe that the colonel, a man of mild appearance and courteous manner, could have been the subject of serious allegations relating to the procuring of young Indian women. He seemed uneasy at our request to visit the reservation, explaining his reluctance by the circumstance that a French couple who had been there on what had been described to him as a scientific mission had filmed Guayakis engaged in sexual intercourse. Their film had been shown in Panama. We assured the Colonel that we had no film cameras with us, and he seemed relieved. A trip might be possible, he said, but we should have to be accompanied by an official from his department. He would also have to obtain the permission of his superior, the minister.

A wait of some days followed, which we filled in with visits to country towns in the neighbourhood of Asunción. Many of these – once early Jesuit settlements – were of great charm, and the grandiose churches of the seventeenth century remain – a superb example being that of Yaguarón, a building of such external severity as to be hardly recognizable as a church, yet which astonishes with the extravagant baroque of its interior, decorated by Indian artists.

The delay provided time for interesting interviews, notably one with the Bishop of the Chaco region, Mgr Alejo Ovelar. The bishop spoke of growing concern felt by churchmen and intellectuals throughout Latin America over the activities of certain missionary sects 'who seem indifferent to the spiritual – let alone material – welfare of the primitive peoples among whom they work, but subject them instead to commercial exploitation'. As a specific example he said that North American missionaries had set themselves up as middlemen in the Chaco region compelling Indians such as the Moros, who lived by hunting and trapping, to sell their skins through the mission. Traders who attempted to deal direct with the Moros had actually been threatened with violence. 'These missionaries,' said the bishop, 'are also implicated in the grave crime of ethnocide.'

In due course, Colonel Infanzón announced his decision. We could go to Cecilio Baez if we were prepared to give an undertaking that any article written about Paraguay would contain no evaluation of the situation of the Indians in that country. Since we proposed to avoid evaluations and deal in facts, not about 'the Indians of Paraguay' as a whole but about the Guayaki, it seemed possible to agree to this. The permit was then given, together with a letter of introduction to Mr Jack Stolz, 'American Missionary in charge at the Colonia Nacionál Guayaki, Cecilio Baez'. The proviso that we should have to be accompanied by an official from the Ministry of Defence had evidently been forgotten. Next morning at six, we set off.

The weather in Paraguay at this season of the year is subject to dramatic variation. Rainfall is at its highest, a sweltering summer is only weeks away, and hurricanes occur. We were being driven by a Paraguayan friend in his Citroën 'Deux Chevaux', and he had warned us that we could reach the reservation only if the rain held off. There are only two paved highways in Paraguay: one from Asunción, to Foz do Iguaçu on the Brazilian frontier, and the other, only about thirty miles in length, to the town of Paraguari, south-east of the capital. All the others are dirt roads, which are closed to traffic by steel barriers as soon as it rains, when the surfaces are instantly transformed into slimy red mud, and makeshift bridges are sometimes carried away. To reach Cecilio Baez we had to cover about 120 miles of the paved highway to Caaguazú and there take a left turning along a dirt road, leading eventually through 50 miles of forest to the reservation. This road was reported to be in exceedingly bad condition.

At Coronel Oviedo, thirty miles short of Caaguazú, clouds were building up ahead, and road police told us that it was raining in eastern Paraguay, and that all the roads were closed. We therefore turned off southwards in the hope of reaching our friend's house in Caazapá. At Villarrica the road was barred, but after delicate and protracted negotiations with the road police, the barrier was unlocked and we were waved on into a landscape veiled already in pearly rain.

In this area all the Arcadian charm, the style and the swagger of South America had survived in its purest form. The streets of small towns like Caacayí (named after the call of a bird) had turned to grassland cropped by cows, and diurnal bats fluttered from the windows of great sepulchral mansions emptied by so many wars and revolutions. Aloof horsemen went thudding past under their wide hats, a palm always upraised in greeting. Enormous blue butterflies floated by – never molested because the Guaranis believe them to be the 'ears of God'. The distances dispensed frugal harp music, and the melodious hoot of the bell-bird. There were eagles in the flowering trees by the roadside, and once we spotted a Model T Ford that had brought a couple to market. Caazapá, reached at sundown – after pushing the Citroën through miles, it seemed to us, of slippery mud – was at the end of the road, and if there was any place in the world to get away from it all, this was it.

In living memory there had been Guayakis in the woods round Caazapá, but it is a quarter of a century since the last of them were cut up to bait jaguar traps, or otherwise killed or enslaved. At San Juan Nepomuceno, twenty miles away, an episode took place in 1949 which proved too much even for the stomachs of the local whites. An Indian hunter called Pichín López managed to round up the last of the Guayakis in the area, and having hacked to death the aged and enfeebled, carried off the viable survivors to San Juan, where, naked and in chains, they were exposed in the town square for public sale. Pichín, denounced by the local priest, had to leave the country. It was the first time that Indian-killing had provoked such disapproval. Pichín's lieutenant at that epoch was none other than Jesús Pereira – twenty years later the government's administrator of the Colonia Guayaki Nacionál at Cecilio Baez.

The present calm of towns such as San Juan and Caazapá conceals undercurrents of extraordinary violence. In 1947 the political boss of Caazapá, one Matilde Villalba – a notable Indian-killer himself in his time – was ambushed and shot down with six of his sixteen sons, and the cemetery at that time being full to overflowing with victims of the short but incredibly bloody civil war just concluded, a charitable neighbour had to lend space in his family vault to accommodate the bodies. Guerrilla fighters captured in the vicinity round about the time of the Che Guevara fiasco in Bolivia were taken straight up and pitched from planes. Remembering this sombre period our friend said, 'Thank God we now have peace and tranquillity.' No sooner had this utterance been made than we noticed several people running to get a better view of something that was happening in the next street. 'It is nothing,' we were assured. 'Probably two men have challenged each other to a duel.' As it happened the excitement was caused by an informally staged bullfight, but confrontations – *High Noon* style – are said to remain common.

Next morning we left Caazapá early and drove all day over officially closed roads and collapsing bridges to reach Caaguazú by evening. The town was under water, and having found beds in a lodging house we splashed through the floods to the nearest cantina for a meal. Here, by the purest chance, a boy of about eight fetching and carrying in the restaurant was pointed out as a slave.

In such cases the child will be passed off as 'adopted', and given the family name, although he will remain in a subservient position in the family for the rest of his days. The boy admitted to me to being an Indian – the family had rather absurdly denied that he was one – and he was clearly delighted by the rare experience of being for once the object of attention.

Incessant rain compelled us next day to return to Asunción, and this, as it turned out later, may have been a good thing. Three days later, a young Englishman employed on a scientific project in Paraguay offered to take us in his Land Rover to Cecilio Baez, and once again we set out at dawn. The reservation, reached through narrow and constantly branching tracks through the partially cleared forest, was hard to find, but eventually we came into a large clearing at the end of which a number of huts clustered round a building which, from its size and style, was clearly the missionary's house.

Several Indians in near rags were mooching about, and a white man in mechanic's overalls tinkered with a piece of machinery. This proved to be Mr Jack Stolz, who received us with marked coolness. I presented Colonel Infanzón's letter, and without lowering his guard, Mr Stolz said that he had expected us three days before. From this it was clear that Colonel Infanzón had been in touch with Cecilio Baez by radio. I explained that we had been held up by the weather, but it was clear that the missionary remained suspicious. He questioned us much in the way that Colonel Infanzón had done, and the occasion seemed a delicate one. I formed the opinion that Mr Stolz would have to be regarded to all intents and purposes as a functionary of the government, empowered to turn us away from the reservation if he thought fit. We gave non-committal replies, but a positive assurance that we had no intention of making indecent movies of the Indians. At this point it turned out that Mr Stolz had never heard of Colonel Infanzón's French couple. Mrs Stolz now came out of the house. Although I would have taken her husband for a top sergeant in an American combat unit rather than a missionary, she was what one thought of as the typical missionary's wife; resolutely smiling, and calm in what might have seemed to her a crisis. She invited us into the house, which was pleasantly furnished without being luxurious, and devoid of the labour-saving gadgetry commonly found in such missionary establishments. Donald McCullin then found an excuse to wander off and start photographing, while I began to attempt to prise the missionary out of a defensive silence that had set in.

I asked Mr Stolz how many Indians were on the reservation, and he said there were 300. Most of them were out working on the land, he said. When I asked if I could see them at work he said they were on their way back to the camp and would be coming in soon. This seemed reasonable enough. It was now nearly noon. In Paraguay the working day starts soon after dawn, and the whole country knocks off for a siesta at midday. Work then recommences at three and continues until sunset. I asked Mr Stolz what the Indians were paid, and after a little hesitation he said they received 100 guaranies (about 33p) a day. 'They have no sense of trade or money,' he said.

In view of the camp's large increase in population since the visit of the *New York Times* correspondent in

January, I thought it reasonable to enquire where the new arrivals had come from. Mr Stolz seemed evasive. They just came in from time to time, he said. 'In the night.' The last group had arrived some weeks previously. He agreed that no 'wild' Guayakis were to be found any longer in the vicinity, and that those recently arrived had come from a long way away. 'What made them come?' I asked, and Mr Stolz said: 'Maybe they heard this was a good place to be in.' He confirmed that there were many enslaved Indian children in the neighbourhood. He mentioned four that had been taken two years previously at Kuruzú some twenty kilometres away, but had not survived. One of these had died from a gun-butt blow received at the time of his capture, and the others shortly afterwards from measles, a disease against which forest Indians have built up no immunity.

'It's the smart thing to own a Guayaki round here,' he said. 'I guess it's a kind of status symbol.'

Donald was anxious to photograph Guayakis playing their musical instruments; their flutes and above all a species of one-stringed fiddle with which a range of about three notes is obtained simply by bending the neck, and thus varying the tension of the string. Mr Stolz said flatly that there were no musical instruments of any kind on the reservation. Did the Indians perform any traditional ceremonies? I asked. No, he said, none. Were there any chiefs? No. Any medicine men? Absolutely not. The only thing the Guayakis ever seemed to do was to sing, he said. The words of their songs were 'not too interesting'. The men were always trying to build themselves up as great hunters, and the women sang those terrible groaning, bellyaching songs. They blamed everything on their ancestors.

At this point I decided to ask Mr Stolz what was the function of the mission and he replied that it was to bring salvation to those who were in a state of sin. This was to be done, eventually, by baptism after the converts had accepted Christ in their hearts, and by 'admission through the mouth'. He thought it was a good thing that I should write down his replies to these questions on topics of faith and conversion and this I carefully did.

How many Guayakis had he baptized? I asked, and Mr Stolz said none. 'Before I can bring them to Christ I must first understand what they believe,' he explained.

'And do you?' I asked him.

Mr Stolz said, 'Vaguely.' He had a problem with the language, he added, but at least he knew that they believed in three gods. The tiger (jaguar), the alligator, and the grandfather. 'This makes things difficult. When we talk of God's son they think of a tiger's son. It's hard to get across the idea they can be redeemed from sin by a tiger's son nailed to a cross. None of these Indians can make the admission, because they do not know what to admit.'

I asked Mr Stolz what progress, if any, had been made towards conversion, and he replied that most of them at least realized that they were living in a state of sin, particularly in sexual matters.

As by Mr Stolz's own estimate it would be many years before any of the Guayakis were brought by his efforts into the fold of Christianity, it was supposed that many in the meanwhile would die, while a few, at least, would probably remain beyond reach of the missionary effort. What in the view of the New Tribes Mission, I asked, would be their spiritual fate?

Mr Stolz was on firm ground now. 'There is no

salvation,' he said, 'for those who cannot be reached. The Book tells us that there are only two places in the hereafter: heaven and hell. Hell is where those who cannot be reached will spend eternity.'

It seemed to me unreasonable that divine retribution should be visited on the Guayakis because Mr Stolz had been unable to learn their language, but the missionary shrugged his shoulders. Such things were beyond his jurisdiction, he suggested. Soon after this he excused himself to return to stripping down an electrical generator, some part of which had to be got away to Asunción that day, and I only saw him briefly again before we left.

I now joined Donald at his photography, noticing by this time that several young missionaries, not in evidence before, had come on the scene. There were about twelve small huts in the immediate area of the mission house. These averaged some fifteen feet square and it was difficult to imagine how as many as 300 Indians could have been sheltered in them. We saw about thirty-five Guayakis in all, about half of them the possessors of skin of the extraordinary waxen whiteness for which anthropologists have been able to offer no explanation. All of them were extremely mongoloid in appearance, and many could have passed for Eskimos. At a rough estimate about fifteen of these were nubile young women, or mothers with babies. There were a half-dozen boys between eight and twelve years of age, and two young girls in this age-bracket, all with the distended stomachs and decayed teeth suggestive of malnutrition. The rest of the visible population was made up of adult males.

All the Guayakis, with the exception of two or three men wearing pseudo-military uniforms, were in dirty cast-offs. There appeared to be no sanitary arrangements in the camp area, which smelled of human excrement. We noted that the adult males had access to bows and arrows with which they showed off their skill to the missionaries. The fact that these men were not at work, and that the missionaries fraternized with them in an affectionate manner, suggested at least the possibility that they were privileged, possibly as camp 'trusties', or even *señuelos*. In common with all other visitors to the reservation we observed an extreme disproportion in the sexes of its population. If Mr Stolz had told us correctly, there were 300 Indians, but – presuming women were not compelled to work with their menfolk on the farms – men outnumbered women by about twenty to one. We found it strange that we should have seen no old men.

About half the Indian adults were lying on the ground in their huts in what seemed a condition of total apathy, giving no evidence of awareness of our presence as we came and went. We saw no signs of food anywhere in the huts – no scraps or left-overs.

Some of the Indians had managed to keep the pets from which they are never parted when at liberty. In one hut we found three tame coatis, in another a fox cub, in another a baby vulture. The little boys with distended stomachs under their filthy shirts who came running up to stroke our hands and caress our fingers (the Guayaki are the most affectionate and outgoing of the Indian races) showed us their tame lizards. One had a hen perched on his shoulder, and another a hawk.

Having finished his photography in the central area of the camp, Donald strolled off towards two huts on the outskirts, followed by Mr Stolz's son, who by now was carrying his tripod, and a smiling young missionary who assured him that there was nothing more to be seen. In one hut he found two old Indian ladies, in the last stages of emaciation and clearly on the verge of death. They lay on the ground apparently having been abandoned to their fate. This was a scene of the kind one associates with the ultimate disasters of Ethiopia and Bangladesh. In the second hut lay a third woman, also in a desperate condition, and Mr Stolz's son, who had come up with the tripod, explained that she had been shot in the side while being brought in.

It was clear that behind the evasions and the resentful silences of Cecilio Baez a great deal remained to be explained before the charges made by the International League for the Rights of Man could be brushed aside. But it was also clear that attempts to probe further, at this time, into what went on behind the scenes would have been futile. Paraguay, the firmest of the Latin American dictatorships, is not a country where it is recommended to put too many inconvenient questions to persons entrusted by the government with the implementation of official policy. We should have been very unhappy indeed, for example, to have been obliged to surrender Donald's films when leaving the country.

But as it turned out, a few more of the facts were let slip by a visiting New Tribes missionary from the Chaco, who asked us when we left – after several hours' fruitless waiting for the Guayakis to come in from the farms – to give him a lift back to Asunción. He had been stranded by the rains for four days at Cecilio Baez, and, convinced that God had sent us in answer to his prayers, in his euphoria and relief he threw caution to the winds.

Mr Stolz had told us that the Indians received 100

guaranies a day (spendable at the mission's store), but the Chaco missionary dismissed this as absurd. The farmers they worked for *promised* them 200 guaranies (66p) a *week*, but more often than not fobbed them off in the end with an old shirt, or a worn-out pair of pants. The Chaco missionary also succeeded in letting the cat out of the bag in the matter of Mr Stolz's activities as an Indian-catcher. He had been out several times recently 'to make contact' he said, and once, indeed, had been narrowly missed by a Guayaki arrow.

It would be impossible without an investigation to substantiate the allegations that have been made that Mr Stolz has engaged in traditional manhunts using *señuelos*, and no investigator is ever likely to be permitted at the camp. But it is clear that the Indian population of Cecilio Baez has much increased in the past few months, and it is hard to believe that free Indians would wish to make a journey of at least 100 miles from the remote forests where they still exist, in order to deliver themselves up to a condition hardly distinguishable from slavery. In fact their reluctance to be 'attracted' by Mr Stolz is very clear from his colleague's account of the arrow that narrowly missed him.

By Mr Stolz's own admission the New Tribes mission at Cecilio Baez performs no religious function. What then is its purpose? It is hard not to agree with the view of Dr Mark Münzel in IWGIA Document No. 17, published in Copenhagen in August 1974, that: 'The reservation has the function of a transitional "taming" camp: the proud and "wild" Indians of the forest would not be immediately willing to work in the white man's fields; but they are willing once they have passed through the reservation, because they see no other solution, or because they are so instructed by the missionaries.' It has seemed strange to outside observers that the countries of Latin America should tolerate and even favour the presence of such North American Protestant missions dispensing – when religious instruction is given at all – a version of Christianity which must be repellent to their own Catholic beliefs. The reason can only be that they are regarded by governments, intent at all costs on the 'development' of natural resources, as efficient in the performance of work that no other organizations are qualified by philosophy, temperament and – above all – by tradition, to undertake.

I do not believe that Mr Stolz would be particularly concerned to defend himself from inclusion in the category of those missionaries who, by the verdict of Bishop Alejo Ovelar, 'are implicated in the grave crime of ethnocide', because he would see nothing wrong in the destruction of the racial identity of Indians for which he feels little but contempt.

'We believe,' says the printed doctrinal statement of the New Tribes Mission, in 'the unending punishment of the unsaved.' What is a few months or even years of misery at Cecilio Baez compared to that?

1975

THE TRIBE THAT CRUCIFIED CHRIST

OUR FIRST VIEW of the Panare was at the village of Guanama, sweltering at the end of the track from an unfinished dirt road that faltered southwards through Venezuela in the general direction of the Amazon. A half-dozen Panare males came out of a communal round-house, moving springily like ballet dancers, with an offering of hot mango juice. They were good examples of a people described as incredibly impervious to Western influence, dressed therefore in no more than scrupulously woven loinclothes, and armlets of blue and white beads. A long ancestry of nomadism had shaped them, and by comparison their nearest white neighbours, who spent their lives on horseback or in cars, seemed awkwardly put together, a little misshapen even, and inclined to fat. The Panare, who could run and walk fifty miles a day across the savannah if put to it, were lean, lithe and supple, coming close in their bodily proportions to the classic ideal.

Guanama was spruce and trim, with everything in place, a little like an anthropological model. Its round-houses were masterpieces of Stone Age architecture, built for all weathers, and marvellously cool under their deep fringing of thatch. It was a quiet place, as Panare villages are wont to be. The dogs remained silent and respectful, children did not cry, and the adults, back from hunting or work in their gardens, slipped into their hammocks after greeting us, to resume soft-voiced discussions on the topic of the day. Only one thing seemed out of place in this calm and confiding atmosphere – the new barbed-wire fence, a symbolic intrusion of an alien point of view.

We had made a point of this visit to Guanama after a report of extraordinary happenings by Maria Eugenia Villalón, who had gone there while employed in a census of the Indian population. A year before she had been in Guanama to record Panare songs, and now, returning for the census, she proposed to entertain the villagers by playing these back to them. No sooner had the tape recorder been switched on than the Indians leapt to their feet in a state of panic, running in all directions, their hands clasped over their ears. The machine was switched off and the commotion subsided. The Panare explained that what they had been compelled to listen to was the voice of the Devil speaking through their mouths. Now they had found Jesus, and henceforward would sing nothing but hymns. They lined up to oblige with one of these, a Panare version of 'Weary of earth and laden with my sin . . .', the first line repeated ad infinitum to Mexican guitars and the rattle of maracas. It was clear to Señora Villalón that the New Tribes Mission had moved in. Members of this organization are the standard-bearers in Venezuela of the new computerized, airborne evangelism that insists not only on conversion, but on the demolition of all those ceremonies and beliefs by which an indigenous culture is defined.

The question now was how far the missionary labours had progressed. Evangelists rush to cover the unclothed human form, and the spectacle of Indians dressed in shapeless and often grubby Western cast-offs is frequently a glum reminder of their presence. Apart from the barbed-wire fence, Guanama was free from the ugliness too often associated with the disruption of belief. We preferred not to abandon hope, and Paul Henley, the British anthropologist who was with us, who has lived, off and on, among the Panare since 1975 and speaks their language fluently, now put the fatal question. 'When is your initiation ceremony to be held?' The reply was a depressing one, confirming our worst fears. 'There will be no ceremony. God is against it. We have turned our backs on all these things.'

It was a breach with the past indeed. The *Katayinto*, the great male initiation ceremony, held in the dry season when food is most plentiful, is for the Panare the culmination of the annual cycle, and to them the equivalent of all the religious and secular feasts of the West rolled into one. Weeks of food-gathering and general preparations are called for, and the festival itself, involving dramatic episodes and three major and a number of minor dances, may stretch over six weeks. It ends with the boys' investiture with the loincloths signifying their attainment of adult status. To the Panare the loincloth represents what the turban does to the Sikhs, and to destroy the *Katayinto* ceremony is to remove the cornerstone and expunge the future of a culture believed by those who have studied it to have developed over thousands of years. No one understands this better than the missionaries, for whom all such ceremonies, and the wearing of the loincloth itself, shackles the Indian – as they see it – to the heathen past. From time to time *Brown Gold*, house magazine of the New Tribes Mission, prints a jubilant notice of a tribe that has been persuaded to change loincloths for trousers, evidence that it is at last on a road from which there is no turning back. Thus in Tanjung Maju: 'The first time we entered the village they were wearing loincloths and very primitive . . . see how they have grown in the Lord.'

The New Tribes Mission, now continuing its implacable advance in those parts of the world where 'uncontacted' tribal people remain to be swept into the evangelical net, was founded in 1941 in El Chico, California, and now has some 1,500 missionaries working with 125 tribes in 16 countries. In South America, which it has divided up with its missionary rival, the Summer Institute of Linguistics, and where it is represented in Venezuela, Bolivia, Brazil and Paraguay, it has rolled over the Catholic opposition. The Catholic Fathers, sometimes reproaching their flock with desertion, are discouraged by the reply, 'You have no aeroplanes. You are not in touch with God by radio.' To the outsider both fundamentalist missions are identical in their aim and the methods employed, but the New Tribes Mission criticizes the Summer Institute of Linguistics as 'too liberal'. Both view Catholics with distaste, and their converts as hardly better placed in the salvation stakes than outright pagans.

Mission finances, according to its prospectus, depend upon public donations. These do not necessarily take the form of cash. Survival International (1980) reports an offering of 2,500 hectares of land by the government of Paraguay, and in 1975 a missionary spoke to me of 'a heck of a piece of land given to the Mission by a company in the Paraguayan Gran Chaco engaged in the extraction of tannin. They figured we could help with the Indians.' The Mission does not hold itself aloof from engaging in commerce, acting frequently as middleman in the supply of goods to the Indians or the resale of their artefacts. Survival International mentions that they are in the fur trade in Paraguay, dealing in jaguar skins, which fetch high prices since the jaguar elsewhere is an internationally protected animal.

Impressive technical equipment and abundant funds give the New Tribes Mission more than a head start in the race for souls. Thereafter its work is carried forward by the zeal of its 'born-again' fundamentalist missionaries recruited from those areas of the United States where Darwin is excluded from the school curriculum, fossils are explained away as Devil's devices implanted in the rocks to cause confusion among the servants of God, and the reappearance of the witches of Salem would cause no great surprise. The Mission proclaims with fervour and enthusiasm the imminent Second Coming of Christ and the destruction of this world, and its doctrinal statement includes the belief in the 'unending punishment of the unsaved', thus committing to the flames of hell all adherents of Judaism, Hinduism, Buddhism and Islam, besides several thousand minor religious faiths and all the great and good men of all races whose misfortune it was to be born before the coming of Christ.

Two thousand tribes remain to be contacted, all of

them under a threat of everlasting fire, so conversion is a task of utmost urgency. It is this sense of time being so short that tends to outweigh all considerations of the convert's welfare in this life, provided that his soul is saved for eternity. 'He saves the souls of men,' runs the New Tribes Mission doctrine, 'not that they might continue to live in the world, but that they might live forever with Him, in the world to come.'

Missionary tactics have undergone little change since the Jesuits first accompanied the Spanish to the conquest of the New World, although they are now reinforced by techniques of persuasion used with success by such sects as the Holy Spirit Association for the Unification of World Christianity under the leadership of the Reverend Moon. The first task is to establish the dependence of the newly contacted native, and this is a matter of invariable routine. Here is a missionary speaking: 'We leave gifts ... knives, axes, mirrors, the kind of things Indians can't resist ... After a while the relationship develops. We have to break their dependence on us next. Naturally they want to go on receiving all these desirable things we've been giving them, and sometimes it comes as a surprise when we explain that from now on if they want to possess them they must work for money ... We can usually fix them up with something on the local farms. They settle down to it when they realize that there's no going back.'

The manoeuvre never fails to work, accomplishing in the end the inevitable tragic result. There's no going back. The trap baited with the fatal gifts is sprung and conversion follows with its long catalogue of prohibitions. The evangelized Indian is forbidden to drink, sing, dance, wear traditional ornaments, paint his body, take part in any of the old ceremonies, marry a non-believing wife. A stern and pleasure-hating deity speaking through the missionary's mouth lists his embargoes, backed by awful descriptions of the lake brimming with fire and brimstone. Too often, 'something on the local farms', whose owners may themselves be close to the poverty line, is hardly distinguishable from slavery, and in the end the detribalized Indian drifts away to his last refuge, the slums of a town where his wife's prostitution provides the money to buy rum and oblivion.

Military dictatorships are the natural supporters of the New Tribes Mission, with whom they share similar views. Les Pederson, a director, illustrates this identity of outlook in his autobiography *Poisoned Arrows*: '... the President of the Republic of Paraguay, don Alfredo Stroessner ... assured me of his appreciation of what we are doing among the indigenous peoples of the country.' Elsewhere efforts to get rid of the missionaries have been frequent, strenuous, and sometimes crowned with temporary success. The clamour has been loudest in Venezuela, where a united front of jurists, anthropologists and churchmen has accused the Mission of infringement of the Indians' human rights, of coercion and forcible conversion. Public opinion has led to the creation of two Congressional investigations. The latter of these opened in 1979, and remained in session for some two years, filling the Venezuelan press with bizarre accounts of missionary goings-on.

Naval Captain Mariño Blanco, charged with keeping an eye on the doings of foreigners in the country's remote regions, spoke of scientific espionage. He noted that the missionaries inevitably installed themselves in areas known to contain strategic minerals such as cobalt and uranium, and claimed to have proved that they were in the pay of American multinationals, naming two of them as Westinghouse and General Dynamics. He noted that the Mission had been in trouble in Colombia, suffering expulsion for 'damage to national interests and for having assisted illicit explorations carried out by transnational companies in areas likely to contain deposits of strategic materials'. The captain had found missionary baggage labelled 'combustible materials' to contain military uniforms and 'other articles' – this being taken by the press to refer to Geiger counters. The uniforms were explained away by the missionaries as intended to impress the Indians. Captain Blanco said that the head of the New Tribes Mission had tried to bribe him. He gave his opinion that the missionaries' involvement with the Indians was only a cover for their other activities.

A Ye'cuana Indian, Simeón Jiménez, speaking defective Spanish with much eloquence, appeared to describe the prohibitions imposed upon his people as soon as the missionaries had taken hold. They included the drinking of fermented juices, dancing, singing, the use of musical instruments, tribal medicines and tobacco, and the tribal custom of arranging marriages within the framework of kinship groups.

Jiménez stressed the psychological terror the Ye'cuanas were subjected to to force them to become converted. In particular he cited the appearance of a comet, described by the chief missionary in the area as heralding the end of the world. The missionary had gathered the Ye'cuanas together and given them three days, on pain of suffering a fiery extinction, to break with their wicked past. They were later warned by the same men of a communist plot to drive the missionaries out of the country, saying that if this were to happen U.S. Airforce planes would be sent to bomb Ye'cuana villages.

I was unable to see Simeón himself and listen to an account of their traumatic experience from his own lips, because he was seven days away by canoe in the Orinoco jungle. Instead I called on his wife, Dr Nelly Arvelo, a distinguished anthropologist who had set a seal on her approval of the life-style of primitive hunters and gatherers by marrying one. She confirmed all her husband had had to say, including an incident when Simeón's aged grandmother had come to him in tears, imploring him to give up his struggle before they were all reduced to ashes.

Terror apart, Dr Arvelo said, the missionaries had worked out a new kind of punishment for those who resisted conversion. 'Indians,' she said, 'like to do everything together. They share everything, particularly their food. They're very close to each other. The missionaries understood this so they worked out that the best way to punish those who didn't want to be converted was by isolation. As soon as they had a strong following in a village they would order the converts to have nothing more to do with those who held out. No one, not even their own parents, was allowed to talk to them, and they were obliged to eat apart from the rest. It was the worst punishment an Indian could imagine, and often it worked.'

Simeón Jiménez was followed into the Congressional hearing by more Indians, some of them discreetly smeared with vermilion as if for a ceremony and wearing loincloths under their trousers, who described what life was like under the thumb of the huge fair-haired men who had dropped into their midst out of the sky. A planeload of converts with short-back-and-side haircuts, baseball caps and bumper boots was flown in from the jungle, but their offer of a hymn session was turned down by the commission. An airforce general who had become a born-again Christian and had worked closely with the New Tribes Mission described Captain Blanco as a crazy fellow who wanted to draw attention to himself, and it was learned that, shortly afterwards, pressure had been brought to bear resulting in Blanco's dismissal from the service.

In the meantime the press had been delving into the Mission's history, noting that in Paraguay they had been involved in manhunts carried out against the Aché Indians and in more manhunts, enforced relocation and enslavement of 'wild' Ayoreos (Survival International, 1980). It was further noted that a description of such an armed manhunt, when Indian fugitives were taken as slaves, had actually appeared in a Mission publication. A group of foreign anthropologists, three of them British, wrote a letter to a Caracas newspaper calling for the Mission's expulsion, and two American signatories were immediately summoned to their embassy to receive an ambassadorial rebuke. According to Captain Blanco there was at least one other intervention by the U.S. Embassy in support of the New Tribes Mission. 'I ordered the arrest of two American engineers named Ward and Curry, who were carrying out (illegal) scientific investigations ... Later it was proved that James Bou (head of the New Tribes Mission in Venezuela) had organized their journey ... Mr Bou telephoned the U.S. Embassy, and the Counsellor of the

Embassy then called me, asking me to release the two men.'

The feelings of the Venezuelans as a whole were summed up by the Apostolic Vicar of Puerto Ayacucho, the Amazonian capital, who said: 'These people have created a terrible confusion in the Indian's mind. They have no conception of Indian culture. When you forbid the Indian to dance, drink his *yarake* or eat the ashes of his dead ones, you destroy his culture. One doesn't spread God's message by terror. The New Tribes Mission relies on force and if the native allows himself to be converted he does so not out of conviction, but fear.'

The methods used by the New Tribes Mission to deal with the Ye'cuana seemed to have proved successful, as a high percentage of the tribe – perhaps as much as 75 per cent – had been induced to accept conversion and to renounce their old customs. Attention was now focused on the Panare, who had been least receptive of all Venezuela's twenty Indian tribes to the evangelical message. Henry Corradini, a Venezuelan anthropologist who has worked with the Panare for a number of years and speaks their language, began an investigation of books of scriptural stories translated by the Mission into the Panare language, which he suspected might have embodied manipulations of the holy text.

In April 1972, a Mr and Mrs Price of the New Tribes Mission had carried out an aerial survey of the Panare region and decided on establishing a mission in the Colorado valley, where an easily accessible Indian settlement had been observed. A jeep was sent to the spot, where they were well received. 'The Lord provided us with a Panare guide, without whom we would not have known where to go.' Although they had been told before that the Panare never worked for anyone, such was the native hospitality that 'the Indians seemed willing to have us come to live there and to build a house for us ... the Panare fellows pitched in and worked really hard.' Clearly there was satisfactory human material for the missionary labours here, and only a small note of disapproval obtrudes. 'On the other side of the clearing could be seen a large, hollowed-out log in which they had their drink, made of mashed corn, sugar cane and sweet potato. The tracks where they had danced were still visible.'

Thereafter progress towards salvation went at a snail's pace. The Indians were helpful and friendly in every way but they had had contacts with missionaries – Jesuits and Franciscans – in the past, and had clearly not enjoyed the experience. Five years after the Lord had 'impressed upon the hearts' of the original three mission-aries to settle where they did, the Panare continued to lead their same old easy-going lives, to drink and to dance, to share their food and do as little work as they had to. They remained eager recipients of trade goods, using the missionaries' iron tools to increase the size of the communal houses the missionaries so much disliked, and of their gardens where far too much of the produce went into the preparation of liquor. In matters relating to the acceptance of the new faith they remained as wary and unreceptive as ever.

Two books based on what purported to be stories from the Bible were soon available in translation, the first *Learning about God* (1975), the second *The Panare Learn About the Devil* (1976). The creation of these had presented certain linguistic problems, solved in the end in a resolute fashion. Difficulties arose from the fact that like many other Indian languages there are no equivalents in Panare for many words held as basic to the concepts of the Christian religion. There are none, for example, for sin, punishment or redemption. God cannot be thanked or praised, only congratulated. Above all, Panare lacks any word for guilt.

This was a situation that had to be rectified. A way had to be found to manufacture the sense of guilt upon which repentance and salvation depended, and the missionary translators may have decided that the best way of tackling this was by re-editing the scriptures in such a way as to implicate the Panare in Christ's death. Henry Corradini soon discovered that the New Tribes Mission's version of the Crucifixion as arranged for Indian consumption was at striking variance with that of the Bible. Gone were the Romans, the Last Supper, the trial and Pontius Pilate turning away to wash his hands. He read on:

> The Panare killed Jesus Christ
> because they were wicked.
> Let's kill Jesus Christ,
> said the Panare.
> The Panare seized Jesus Christ.
> The Panare killed in this way.
> They laid a cross on the ground.
> They fastened his hands and his feet
> against the wooden beams, with nails.
> They raised him straight up, nailed.
> The man died like that, nailed.
> Thus the Panare killed Jesus Christ.

If this could not create feelings of guilt, nothing could.

Now there was talk of God's vengeance for the dreadful deed.

> *God will burn you all,*
> *burn all the animals, burn also the earth,*
> *the heavens, absolutely everything.*
> *He will burn also the Panare themselves.*
> *God will exterminate the Panare*
> *by throwing them on to the fire.*
> *It is a huge fire.*
> *I'm going to hurl the Panare into the fire,*
> *said God.*

The comet had come and gone but the frightening memory of it remained. God had relented once but might not a second time.

> *God is good.*
> *Do you want to be roasted in the fire?*
> *asks God.*
> *Do you have something to pay me with*
> *so that I won't roast you in the fire?*
> *What is it you're going to pay me with?*

The nature of the payment demanded is a foregone conclusion; unquestioning submission to the missionaries' demands, the abandonment of their traditional life and their customs, their culture. The pressure proved too much even for the well-tried nerves of the Panare, and within months the first results began to come in. The following, headed 'Panare Breakthrough', is quoted from *Brown Gold*, dated 1977: '... I finished stressing the need for each one to ask God for the payment of their own sins ... A few hours later Achen (a Panare woman) came by the house, she said, "I asked God like this: I want my payment for my sin (sic). I don't want to burn in the big fire. I love Jesus."

'... Here we had sat for almost a year teaching one believer and nothing else happened and then all of a sudden, WOW!'

The Colorado valley, where it had all started, came as a surprise. It gave a feeling of being in the Orient rather than the West, a landscape sketched in briefly by a Chinese artist, red earth with angular trees set among immense black boulders, backed by a recession of low hills afloat in the mist. Communal houses showed among the trees down by the river like delicately woven straw hats, and we could see the Panare women moving about, walking with quick, strutting steps, and wearing nothing but G-strings, tassels and beads. The course of the river was marked by a tight border of forest, full of noisy birds and great dark, blundering butterflies. In this arcadian setting the missionary building, solid and rectangular at the head of the airstrip, seemed austere and aloof.

Paul Henley presented us to the thirty-two adult men and women of the extended family who had adopted him. We had brought gifts for them all, and in accordance with egalitarian principles each man received an identical nylon fishing line, and each woman a garishly decorated enamel bowl. In addition we handed over a sack of rice in return for our share in communal meals we might be invited to join. We were then directed to hang our hammocks in an empty house at the highest point of the village, recommended as being relatively free from mosquitoes. It was a traditional thatched construction, well swept and free in Panare style from litter of any kind. Following a perfunctory inspection to make sure that there were no rattlesnakes about we installed ourselves. Soon after, Panare of all ages and both sexes began their visits, examining and commenting in soft, clucking monosyllables on our persons and our equipment, dropping into unoccupied hammocks, and just standing about in companionable groups long after darkness had fallen, clearly trying to make us feel at home.

Next day the news, as in Guanama, turned out to be discouraging. Two years before when the *Katayinto* ceremony was last held, it had been truncated by the omission of its most dramatic component: a piece of theatre involving the ritual appearance at the height of the dancing by a group of strangers who behave in a hostile and menacing manner, but who are finally pacified and induced to join in the general merriment. This episode seemed to symbolize the young initiates' necessity for arriving at a pacific arrangement with the threatening outside world. The Panare said that they had been obliged to cut it out 'because God did not like it'.

In the following year, 1982, there had been no initiation ceremony at all, and Paul had assumed that this had been no more than a postponement. Now we were to hear that again God had raised objections, and that the *Katayinto* would not take place once more, although it 'might' be held next year. It seemed likely that the missionaries' strategy was to encourage indefinite postponement. The Mission had been careful to keep a low profile while the Congressional investigation was going on. Now there were signs it was moving to the counter-attack. In February 1982, Elizabeth Stucky, one of the missionaries at Colorado, wrote in *Brown Gold*: 'On the surface it seems as though they (the Panare) have the least interest in spiritual things.' She defends current Mission strategy, anticipating the possibility of the American evangelists' eventual expulsion. 'Santos Casanova is one of the six men who Maurice was teaching . . . and who in turn teaches his own people. His group is the largest in the valley who meet together, numbering 100.' This suggests that about half the Panare of Colorado have been evangelized, and if it is true, the *Katayinto* is at an end. Maria Villalón described a native evangelist, trained perhaps by Mr Stucky, at work in a remote Panare community they had visited by helicopter for the census. 'The village children were made to kneel down in a row. No one could understand what was going on, nor could the Panare evangelist make them understand. In the end he said, "every time I say the word Jesus, you must bang your head on the ground", and this they did.'

In the past it had been possible to organize what the Panare call a 'for nothing', a watered-down version of the *Katayinto*, devoid of any ritual significance – certain to have called down the missionaries' ban. The Panare stage a 'for nothing' whenever they can, purely because they like to drink and dance, and they can normally be induced to go through a full repertoire of dances if provided with a sack of sugar with which to brew the very mild, sweet beer obtainable from only three days' fermentation. In preparation for this, a day or so is spent in cutting down a tree and hollowing out from it the 'canoe' to contain the beer – in itself a traditional community exercise in which everyone takes part, and seen as contributing to the fun. We asked if a 'for nothing' could be arranged, but there was always a doubt at the back of the mind. The first sign of fermentation can be detected in a warm climate in any sweetened juice only hours after it has been exposed to the air, and we had heard of native 'deacons' keeping a stern watch to see that all such drinks were jettisoned as soon as the first bubbles appeared on the surface.

While this proposal was under consideration we settled down to give the Panare the chance to get to know us, and to familiarize ourselves with the village scene.

Missionary propaganda has taken a new turn recently, assuring us that peoples not reached by their message have a miserable time in this world as well as being doomed to perdition in the next. 'In the Panare way of life before the Gospel was shared with them, everything was bad. It was their way of life to expect the worst. Misfortunes hung over their heads. Constant fears were always in their hearts. This ever-present fear seems to be the very pulsation of life itself.' Thus Mrs Linda Myers, writing about our hosts shortly before our visit.

All that we saw of them ourselves or from the enquiries made presented a strikingly less dismal picture. We had previously noticed that the Indians' physique was superior to that of the local whites, and now it seemed likely that they enjoyed better health in general. A number of families had produced six or more children, all of whom seemed lively and intelligent. I heard of a man of eighty-two waiting for a thirteen-year-old girl to reach puberty before claiming her as his bride, and no one doubted that there would be issue of the union. By way of comparison a newspaper assured us that a prosperous white had one chance in three of dropping dead by the time he reached fifty. The Panare claim that before introduced diseases such as influenza, measles and malaria took their toll, they suffered from no illnesses at all. Their mental health appeared equally robust. The close-knit communal life of the Panare protects them from most of the pressures familiar in our society, and the crime rate is nil.

The missionaries supply tools and consumer goods to the Panare which have to be paid for in cash. Aspirin and penicillin are now driving out effective remedies derived from local plants, and Western medicines cost money. Sales promotions, sometimes divinely backed, can seem unnecessary; one in particular infuriated Henry Corradini, who had now joined us. 'God wants us to use soap. He wants us to eliminate unpleasant odours; to wash under the armpits and round the anal area.' Corradini said, 'The Indians are never out of the water. Without exception they're the cleanest people in the world. How dare these gringos tell them they stink?'

Cash for these purchases has to be found, so the Panare make decorative baskets which they sell to the local whites. It was part of an evangelical manoeuvre to settle the Indians in the vicinity of the missions, wean them away from the barter system, persuade them to buy more and more inessential goods, converting them in this way into wage-earners working a 48-hour week. It has been calculated that with all their household, horticultural and other chores, the Panare work on average only three hours a day, and the missionary effort to rescue them from the evil effects of sloth has in this case misfired, for basket-weaving is easily done while lying in a hammock, in a state of the almost trance-like Panare reverie.

In other directions the irresistible bait of trade-goods, of fish-hooks, hunting-knives, axes and aluminium bowls has done its work, for the old nomadic expeditions in search of fresh hunting grounds have become fewer and fewer, and this in turn has wiped out stocks of game and fish in the vicinity of Colorado. This being the case, the Panare are always on the lookout for someone with transport who may be cajoled into giving them a lift on a hunting trip to an area which can no longer be reached on foot in a single day.

We took six Indians in the back of the Toyota Land Cruiser deep into the endless park of the savannah in search of mangoes. The fruit-bearing trees could be picked out in the little spinneys dotted about the grassland by the almost artificial brilliance of their foliage among the delicate lavenders and greys of savannah trees. When the Indians spotted them they jumped down, cut bamboos and stirred the branches to dislodge fruit, touching off explosions of toucans and parakeets which streaked away squawking into the sky.

An inclination to keep on the best possible terms with the Panare, with the hope of the 'for nothing' in mind, compelled us to agree with the suggestion they next put up, which was a major fishing expedition which would involve poisoning a stretch of river. This would be done by the use of *enerima*, a liana growing in the mountains which is pounded up and added to the water. The whole idea is a little repellent from the viewpoint of the West, but sporting restraints are meaningless in the context of primitive food-gathering realities, where no one kills for the fun of it but simply to eat. Fishing for pleasure is unknown in the outback of such countries as Venezuela, and insofar as the town-dweller eats fish at all, it is frozen and imported. Consequently the rivers remain stocked, probably to capacity, and when the flow virtually ceases in the dry season, pools form in which stranded fish are confined in an ever-shrinking volume of water, where they are preyed upon by fishing eagles and otters. In this season alone, the Indian uses his poison. His evolution has made a conservationist of him, although he remains unaware of the fact.

It took a day to find and cut the *enerima* and next morning we set out for the Tortuga River, a tributary of the Orinoco, at its nearest point about thirty miles away. The Toyota was crammed, as before, with Panare, but a large number had set out before us on veteran bicycles purchased through the missionaries, with the message 'Christ is coming' painted on the mudguards. On these, pedalling furiously across the savannah, their arrival coincided roughly with ours.

The pool chosen was some 100 yards long by 20 in width. Shoals of kingfishers as big as starlings were splashing into the water when we arrived. Some fifty Panare lined both banks while the poison was being pounded up and put into baskets which were rinsed into the water.

Within five minutes of a milk whiteness spreading into the pool a greater subaqueous commotion began, a spinning catherine wheel of tin-plate reflections just beneath the surface, from which a big fish sometimes spun away then shot off in a straight line, dorsal fin cutting the water, making for the shallows. Occasionally one broke surface, launched itself into the air, thumped down on the bank, then propelled itself in a series of leaps a dozen feet across dry land. The Panare waited for the fish to slow down then speared them phlegmatically and without obvious effort, striking home with their barbed lances at thirty feet or more, and always clean through the head.

Fishing, Stone Age style, was sensationally productive. In less than two hours several hundred fish had been taken, among them 25-pounders, and the total weight of the catch was in the neighbourhood of a ton. A few remained in the pool twisting and turning beyond easy reach, and the Panare said that these would recover in about four hours. *Enerima* seems to be a nerve poison of a sort, for it has no effect upon edibility. The fish were cleaned on the spot, and the first caracara – a spruce and elegant hawk that stands in here for the vulture – dropped from the sky to attend to the clearing-up. The only problem remaining was to get the fish back to the village, where it would immediately be smoked on the many frames already prepared, after which it could be kept some weeks before consumption. It was a highly successful occasion. And the Panare showed pleasure in their usual restrained way. One convert triumphantly produced a tract from the folds of his loincloth – although he was clearly muddled as to the nature of its message, headed, 'Has life nothing better to offer than this?'

The missionaries, with whom it might have been enlightening if not useful to discuss the matter of a 'for nothing', and of a reported ban on photography, were not at home to callers during our first two days in Colorado, and on the third day a plane came and carried them away. Thereafter the mission remained empty, but there was little doubt that evangelical interests were entrusted to their trainee 'deacons' who would report on all happenings.

We had never felt over-optimistic about the 'for nothing' and were resigned now on being told that it could not be arranged after all. The excuse given was that a number of essential participants were about to leave on a trip to the mountains to collect tonka beans, for sale to the whites who used them to add fragrance to tobacco.

Following this setback there was nothing further to keep us at Colorado, and we set out on our return to Caracas. On the way we made a side trip to a diamond-mining camp, attracted there by its name, Tiro Loco (Crazy Shot), and by the news of a recent settlement on its outskirts by Panare who had come down from their forests to taste what was to be had of the joys of civilization in the form of trade-goods.

Tiro Loco prided itself on being tough. It was straight out of Chaplin's *Gold Rush*, a shanty town built on a stratum of crushed beer cans, full of hatchet-faced villains in big hats and spectacular whores. In Tiro Loco you could actually see the swing-doors of a bar fly open and an unwanted customer pitched through them head first into the street.

The mild, calm Panare newcomers had built their round-houses (the best examples seen) on a hillock above this dynamic scene, and the hard men of our times and the peaceful ones representing the distant past had got together to establish an easy-going and mutually satisfactory relationship. Food for the miners, apart from what the Panare had to offer, had to be flown in at great cost, most of it not worth eating when it arrived. The Panare grew excellent vegetables which they were very happy to offer in exchange for gardening tools from the store, or made up easily enough by the miners, if necessary, from the wrecked machinery and devastated cars cluttering Tiro Loco's waste spaces.

This Panare village was one of the few as yet unreached by the New Tribes Mission, and here the Indians lived happily under the protection and patronage of as hard-bitten a selection of humanity as it would have been possible to find. The miners supplied them with all they needed, with no strings attached. In Tiro Loco the Panare could drink, dance, paint themselves and perform their ceremonies to their hearts' content.

The Congressional committee investigating the New Tribes Mission failed to reach any positive conclusion, nor amazingly was its report ever made public. Inevitably the born-again Christian general had described them as a geopolitical necessity, by which he meant it was useful for Indians in remote jungle areas to be under the control of people who were so far politically to the right that they classified all their opponents, archaeologists, journalists, army officers, the Apostolic Vicar of Puerto Ayacucho alike, as communists, but this carried no weight with public opinion. Charges of espionage were held to be unproven. The Mission hardly bothered to defend itself against those of ethnocide, since in its doctrinal statement and its literature it made it abundantly clear that – presented under another name – this was precisely its goal.

Venezuela, since the passing of the dictatorship, has the best human rights record of the countries of South America, and it is inconceivable that a country which accords the right of the freedom of religious beliefs to its white citizens should deny this primal right to its Indians. In April 1982, a missionary couple – the husband had been arrested and charged with illegal actions on two previous occasions – were told to pack up and go. Then in July of last year *Brown Gold* announced that the Department of Justice had stated that no fresh visas would be granted to evangelical missionaries.

If, as seems possible, this means that the end of the New Tribes Mission's domination of the Indians is in sight, the Venezuelan Department of Justice will undoubtedly pay close attention to the fact that the Mission has prepared the ground for just such an emergency, leaving native evangelists implanted in every tribe whose task it will be to carry on the ethnocidal work.

1983

SURVIVING WITH SPIRIT

OF ALL THE great cities Naples has suffered least at the hands of that destroyer of human monuments, the dark angel of Development. Pliny himself, who once stood on a headland there to watch the great eruption of Vesuvius 'shaped like a many-branching tree' in the moment of the obliteration of Pompeii, would have little difficulty in picking out the landmarks of our times. Nor would Nelson and his Emma, who chose roughly the same viewpoint to watch the eruption of their day – nor, certainly, Casanova looking down from his gambling house over the layered roofs and the soft-yellow walls of volcanic *tufa* which hoard and dispense the special Naples sunshine. Hardly a stone of Santa Lucia has been disturbed (except by air-bombardment) since its celebration in the ballad of the 1890s. When the traveller of the last century was adjured to 'See Naples and Die', it was notwithstanding the competition offered by so many glittering rivals. How much more valid and enticing is the invitation now that so many of them have withdrawn into their shells of concrete.

Naples is a once-capital city, glutted with the palaces and churches of the Kingdom of the Two Sicilies. Seen from the heights above it, it is a golden honeycomb of buildings curved into a sea which, beyond a bordering of intense pollution, is as brilliant and translucent as any in the world. It is built on ancient lava fields, and has been threatened by numerous eruptions – only one of which, in 1855, came near to engulfing it: it was saved by the miraculous intervention of a statue of its patron saint, San Gennaro, on the Maddaloni Bridge, spreading its marble arms to halt the passage of the lava. Its history abounds with similar marvels, all of them attested to and recorded by responsible citizens of the day: a plague of mermaids, figures in Giotto's frescos in the Castel dell'Ovo, so marvellously drawn that they were actually seen to move and, more recently, the prodigies performed by Padre Pio, the flying monk, who flew from an outer suburb to the rescue of Italian pilots shot down in combat with Allied planes, bearing them safely to earth in his arms. Dependably in March of every year the dried blood of San Gennaro liquifies in its ampoule in the Cathedral – the most hallucinatory of spectacles surviving from the Middle Ages.

It is characteristic of Naples, described by Scarfoglio as 'the only Oriental city having no resident European quarter', that one of its kings, Ferdinand I, should not only have delighted to play the hurdy-gurdy but have commissioned Haydn to compose six nocturnes on the instrument. He was the ruler of a people infatuated with music, and there is music still, everywhere in the Neapolitan air. There can be few more poetic experiences in the local manner than to visit the Parco della Rimembranza, where the young of the city go to make love in their cars, and to clamber down the cliff to the point where, the passing fishing boats still out of sight, they can be tracked by the trail of their mandolin music on their way out to sea.

Naples has been taken by a long succession of foreign conquerors, the cruellest of them Lord Nelson, who collaborated in the fearsome slaughter of the city's liberals; and possibly the most corrupt the Allies in the last war, who virtually handed over civic control to the American gangster Vito Genovese, in the guise of adviser to the Allied Military Government – an experience from which the city has never wholly recovered. A continuing resistance to so many alien conquerors has sharpened the native capacity for self-defence, and, since few of the laws Neapolitans are subjected to are of their own making, they have a tendency to mistrust law in general. They are gregarious and gay, with a frank devotion to the pleasures of the table and bed. In the last war, Naples was almost certainly the only city in a theatre of warlike operations where civilian employees of our armed forces could apply for transport facilities to their homes at *noon*, to enable them to fulfil their marital obligations.

Cities remain as wonderfully unchanged as Naples is, not from any compunction aroused by their charms in the breasts of the developers but because, for one or another reason, they see no hope of a return on their money. The economy of Naples is chronically ailing and slides from one crisis to another. It is generally accepted that an expanded tourist industry could be its salvation, but the tourists do not come. Some of the reasons why it fails to entice foreigners to break their journey on their way to Sorrento or Amalfi and spend a night or two in its half-empty hotels were listed in *Il Mattino* last year. Sorrowfully the newspaper admitted that Naples had become the home-town of petty criminality. In the past twelve months, 77,290 minor crimes had been reported, but in only 1,300 cases had arrests been made or the criminals even been identified. During this period 29,000 cars had been stolen in the city – possibly a world record taking into account the number of vehicles registered. The Vespa-mounted *scippatori*, the Black Knights of the alleyways, buzzing in and out of the crowds in search of a camera or handbag to snatch, had become so common-place a sight as hardly to evoke notice, interest or comment.

From a glance at the newspaper's statistics it seemed, too, that an evening meal out was to be recommended neither to the native citizen nor the visitor to Naples, since fourteen leading restaurants had been raided by bandits in the past twelve months. It was the kind of experience most of us would want to avoid, but a Neapolitan friend involved in a hold-up had been stimulated rather than alarmed. He had been invited to Da Pina's for a christening celebration. A nice party, he said. The best of everything, with the wine flowing like water. But about half-way through the proceedings three hooded men carrying sawn-off shotguns had walked in and ordered the guests to lie face down on the floor. He was impressed with their courtesy, their correct use of the language, and by the way they addressed their victims using the polite *lei* rather than the familiar *tu*. All in all, it was a bit of an adventure, he said, and well worth the trifling £4 or so he had been obliged to part with. His only fear had been that by some incredible mischance the police might show up and start a battle, as they had done at Lombardi's Pizzeria last June, when fifteen customers were wounded.

But most of the coups pulled off by the organized gangs, the Camorra, which imitate the Mafia of Sicily, are theatrical rather than violent. Three robbers who succeeded in sealing off Parker's Hotel from the outside world, and who took two hours to ransack it from top to bottom, prepared and consumed a leisurely meal before departing.

The recent capture of the Ischia ferry-boat was another episode that might have been modelled on a film; having despoiled the passengers with the now familiar show of civility and regret, the bandits leapt to the deck of a following motor-launch waving farewells and blowing kisses to the girls before vanishing into the night.

If one has an affection for such movies as *The French Connection*, this is an environment not wholly without its own brand of attraction. What in its way can be more pleasant than to draw a chair out on to the balcony of a room in the Hotel Excelsior overlooking the exquisite small harbour of Santa Lucia, and there, glass in hand and without the slightest risk to one's safety and comfort, play the part of an extra in such a film? The view is of the majestic fortress of the Castel dell'Ovo, dominating a port scene by a naïve painter: simple fishermen's houses that have become restaurants, painted boats, tiny, foreshortened maritime figures, going nowhere in particular, a quayside stacked with the pleasant litter of the sea.

There is less innocence in the prospect than at first meets the eye, because a corner of the port has been taken over by a fleet of some forty large motor-launches, painted the darkest of marine blues, devoid of all trappings, and having about them an air of sinister functionalism. From time to time one starts up with a tremendous chuckle of twin 230 Mercury engines, is manoeuvred in swaggering fashion round the other boats and out of the port before, a moment later, trailing a wake like a destroyer, it heads for the horizon.

This is the fleet of the best-organized and most successful *contrabandisti* in southern Italy, and in these launches (which give the impression of having been specially designed for the trade) are smuggled in the cigarettes and who knows what else picked up in incessant rendezvous with the ships steaming out from the ports of Tunisia. Smuggling is hardly the word to describe these operations, all stages of which, taking place in Italian waters, are on open display. The boats come and go throughout the day, unload their cargoes without concealment and cut a few jubilant capers in the harbour before tying up. There are no signs of the law in the harbour area, and motor-cycle policemen passing through Santa Lucia do so hurriedly with eyes averted. Understandings have clearly been reached at high levels. Customs launches lack the speed to catch the *contrabandisti* at sea, and rarely dare to enter the port. Occasional disagreements among the smugglers themselves can, however, be explosive: hotel guests a week or so before our arrival had a ringside seat at a brief battle, followed by a spectacular incineration of boats.

It is a situation viewed by Neapolitans with tacit approval if not with enthusiasm, and the benefits of the direct trade with north Africa to the man in the street are immediately visible. There is hardly a street without a small boy seated at a table to offer Marlboro cigarettes, made in Tunis (only the government health-warning is missing), at less than 500 lire as opposed to the 800 lire charged in the shops. The authorities seem to regard the traffic as hardly more than an inevitable evil. 'I refuse to admit that this is a crime,' said Maurizio Valenzi, the communist Mayor of Naples. 'For me it is an illegal solution.' The mayor shared the frequently voiced Neapolitan view that his city is the victim of a calumnious outside world. 'If you are looking for crime on a big scale, go to Rome or Milan,' he said. 'The worst thing that can happen to you here is to have your pocket picked. Nobody gets mugged in Naples and we treat women with respect. Whoever heard of a Neapolitan being pulled in for knocking a child about? Even the Red Brigade don't operate here.'

Valenzi is as Neapolitan as Brezhnev is Muscovite, lively of expression and gesture, a distinguished painter and a first-rate oratorical performer in a country in which no politician can survive without the knack of rhetoric and a powerful voice. His appearance recalls the views on matters of dress held by Togliatti, party leader for so many years: 'What pleases me is to see a comrade dressed in a good double-breasted suit – if possible, dark blue.' Valenzi is wholly congruous in the rococo furnishings, the marble and the glitter of the Naples Town Hall. He is fired by local patriotism, impatient of criticism of his city, and particularly saddened by those contained in a book by a communist author, Maria Antoinetta Macciocchi, who had been a parliamentary candidate for one of the poor quarters of the city. 'She wasn't much liked here,' the mayor said.

Macciocchi had mentioned that the rat population of central Naples was 7 million. Many of these, she said, were shared out in the *bassi*, those claustrophobic dwellings consisting of a single room that line the streets of the old town, in which as many as fifteen members of a family may live as best they can with no windows, the street doors shut at night, no running water and a closet behind a curtain. The mayor, who showed a partiality for euphemism, shied away from the word *bassi*, but agreed that 69,000 families lived in 'unhygienic houses'. 'The municipality,' he said, 'has plans to do something.'

'Our submerged economy' was Valenzi's description for the child labour existing in Naples to an extent found nowhere else in the Western world. There is no way of calculating the number of children from the age of eight upwards employed in cafés, bars, or the innumerable sweat-shops tucked away in the narrow streets; but there are certainly tens of thousands of them. It would appear to be another 'illegal solution'. Naples has the highest birth-rate in Italy – twice the national average – and it is an everyday accomplishment for a woman to have borne ten children by the age of thirty-five and to have completed a brood of fifteen or sixteen by the time she ceases to reproduce. Such families are a source of complacency rather than despair. One is assured that they testify to a woman's sexual attraction and her husband's virility. More importantly, perhaps, they represent an insurance policy against economic disaster. When up to five or six children contribute small regular sums to the budget a family is not only more affluent but securer than a less numerous one in the trap of chronic unemployment.

These are the facts of Neapolitan life against which Mayor Valenzi struggles like Canute against the waves. If the child in proletarian Naples is an economic weapon in the family armoury it follows as a consequence that such central areas of the city as the Vicaria district have the highest population density in Europe – possibly in the world – with up to three people occupying every two square *metres*. But if overcrowding, and its damaging effect on public health, is the most pressing problem that face the mayor and his council, it is the terrific anachronism of child labour with its whiff of early-Victorian England that gives the city a bad name. Therefore gestures have to be made, and from time to time the police are ordered into action to close down all establishments employing child labour and to punish their owners with exemplary fines. What follows is economic disaster for all involved – sometimes desperate impoverishment for the families thrown back on the providing power of the father who, statistically speaking, can expect to spend a third of his life unemployed. At this point the exploiters and the exploited only too often join forces in protest, and their votes are lost to whatever party is held responsible for their plight.

How is this situation to be tackled? How can any political party hope to put an end to the Neapolitan tradition of the large family which engenders the poverty which is to be fought by even larger families? Schooling in Italy is compulsory up to fourteen years of age, but the school inspectors are as helpless as the politicians. The little courtyards tucked away everywhere in Naples are full of small boys aged upwards of eight years who work ten or twelve hours a day, for as little as £2 a week, stitching and glueing shoes. A happier-looking, more intelligent collection of children it would be hard to find in the family atmosphere that pervades even the workshop. None of them will ever read or write.

* * *

Naples sharpens the stranger's wits and teaches him to look after himself. The lesson is not a difficult one to learn, and in a matter of hours, days at most, amusement is apt to take over from indignation. One exchanges laughter with the agreeable young man who offers a perfect imitation of a Seiko watch that only ticks for a minute or two when it is wound up; or points without severity, on taking a taxi, to the meter inevitably still registering the fare clocked up by the last passenger. There are basic precautions to be taken: passports and valuables are automatically committed to the hotel's safe, and only enough money carried to meet immediate requirements. When parking a car it is not a bad idea to secure the steering wheel with a chain and padlock. These things attended to, one can relax and join in the local games.

Our own arrival in Naples was on the second day of the ancient and popular feast of Santa Maria del Carmine, held in the streets adjacent to the old church at the far end of the port. Del Carmine is the parish church of one of a number of districts, once virtually separate villages. Each has its history, traditions, customs – and often the enfeebled remnant of a once-powerful ruling family. And such was the spirit of rivalry between one district and another that fifty years ago intermarriage between districts was rare.

The church possesses a picture of a 'black' Virgin, held responsible for many cures, in particular of epileptics and lepers and of those afflicted with all kinds of pox. The most unusual and attractive feature of the *festa* is the 'burning' of the church tower, by the setting alight of bales of straw fastened to its walls, with the intention of cleansing it, and thus the district itself, of evil spirits during the forthcoming year. It was a disappointment to learn that the tower was not to be 'burned' on this occasion: repairs to its structure had been found necessary, and the scaffolding was already in place. The cancellation of the ceremony had cast a certain gloom over the neighbourhood, which depends largely on fishing and feared that catches might be affected.

The Corso Garibaldi, a wide if dishevelled street running past the church, was filled by early evening with a holiday crowd. Here all the familiar ingredients of a Neapolitan *festa* were assembled: the stalls with tooth-cracking nougat, solid cakes and cheroots; the shooting booths; the intimidating display of strange shell-fish; balloons and holy pictures – and black-market cigarettes.

In Naples the cult of the enormous Japanese motor-cycle has arrived and they were here in fearsome concentration, roaring through whatever space they found among the press of human bodies. We saw one elfin girl mounted on a Kawasaki 'King Kong' hyper-bike. Children are not over-protected in Naples. The minimum age for a Vespa rider seemed to be twelve or thirteen; and crash helmets were absolutely out.

These are the occasions when, in holiday mood, Neapolitans resolutely suspend belief. A professional 'uncle from Rome' was pointed out to us, aloof and immaculate in his dark suit, ready to hire himself to any family wishing to impress its guests on an occasion such as a christening, wedding or funeral. *Magliari* – confidence tricksters who flock to all such *festas* – were there in numbers, instantly recognizable even to an outsider by the apparatus of their trade.

The grade-A hoax operator presents himself as a rejected suitor offering the 'silver' service bought for the wedding that will no longer take place. *Magliari* in truck-drivers' overalls and with oil on their fingers flog trashy radios and defective tape-recorders 'off the back of the van'. A local boy in burnous and headcloths, skin yellowed by several layers of instant-tan, hawks vile carpets which, he claims, have been brought over from Tunisia with the cigarettes. How do Neapolitans – those masters of guile – allow themselves to be taken in?

Until two years ago the seller of Acqua Ferrata would have been here. This most esteemed and expensive of curative waters, nauseatingly flavoured with iron, was drawn from a hole in the ground somewhere in Santa Lucia and offered – exactly as illustrated in the Pompeii frescos – in containers shaped like a woman's breast. Since then, following a typhoid scare, the health department has stepped in and Acqua Ferrata is at an end – temporarily, perhaps – to be replaced with a poorish substitute: fresh lemonade animated with bicarbonate of soda.

One figure alone from the remote past had survived at del Carmine: the *pazzariello*, the joker of antiquity, also shown in the Pompeii frescos. Once he drove out devils, and as recently as the time of the last war no new business could be opened before a *pazzariello* had been called in to lash out with his stick at every corner of a building where a devil might have concealed himself. The office was an honoured one, hereditary and indispensable, too, in a city where even now people cross the road in the Via Carducci to avoid passing too close to a building notoriously under the influence of the evil eye. But now the magic power of the *pazzariello* has drained away; the one we saw, doing his best to dodge the motorcyclists as he capered about in the Corso Garibaldi, was there to advertise a fish restaurant.

Our visit to del Carmine provided a mild adventure. Among the exhibition of holy pictures, most of them crude versions of the celebrated ikon on display in the church, we noted one of a strikingly different kind; a portrait of a somewhat stolid-looking middle-aged man, stiff in a formal suit: *Il Santo Dottore Moscati*. It turned out that the holy doctor was a GP of the district, recently deceased and newly canonized by popular acclamation, without reference to Vatican or Church, as a result of a number of miraculous cures he had effected.

The display with its new, popular saint seemed to call for a photograph, but the elderly lady in charge fought shy of the camera and retreated in haste, shielding her face with one of the ikons and leaving her husband to conduct any further negotiations. The old man made no objection to being photographed when we agreed to buy a picture of Dr Moscati. Since the light was already failing, the camera was set up on a tripod and the preparations put in hand. Immediately a crowd began to collect, drawn by the powerful magnet of this performance from the competing attractions of a shooting booth and the church just across the road. A Neapolitan friend who had guided us to the *festa* became concerned, feeling that we were attracting too much attention and were too vulnerable, surrounded by photographic gear, to a passing *scippatore*. But the crowd was co-operative and affable; working Neapolitans, as gregarious as pigeons, love nothing better than a new face and an excuse to exchange a smile with a foreigner. People were actually jostling each other and manoeuvring to be included in the photograph, so that, realizing that we were among friends, all warnings were ignored and the photography went ahead.

A moment later there was a sudden chill in the atmosphere and the smiles faded. A grim-faced, gesturing man had pushed himself to the front to demand payment of 50,000 lire – about £30. His story was that he was acting for the owner of the pictures; but it was to be supposed that he was an enforcer of one of the protection gangs said to levy a toll on most Neapolitan business enterprises. We decided to resist the extortion: there were four of us, and we were certain that we had the crowd on our side. The situation was saved when the old man had the courage to admit that he had never seen the presumed gangster before in his life. With this, the unwelcome stranger went off, and the emergency was at an end.

In 1943–44 I spent a year in Naples, arriving a day or so after its capture from the Germans in October 1943, when the city lay devastated by the hurricane of war. The scene was apocalyptic. Ruins were piled high in every street and in these people camped out like Bedouin in a wilderness of brick, on the verge of starvation and close to dying of thirst: there had been no water supply since the great Allied air-bombardment a month before. Families experimented with seawater to cook herbs and edible roots grubbed up in gardens and parks. Some squatted by the shore with weird contraptions with which they hoped to distil seawater to drink. At the same time an absurd and disastrous ban on fishing kept the boats from going out, and children by the hundred were to be seen scrambling about the rocks, prizing off limpets to sell at a few lire a pint, supplies of winkles and sea-snails having been long exhausted. All the rare and extraordinary fish from all parts of the world in the famous aquarium had been eaten by the populace, and a manatee, the aquarium's most prized possession, preserved for a while only by its ugliness, had finally been slaughtered and disguised in the cooking to be served at a banquet in honour of General Mark Clark.

Men and women who had lost all their possessions in the bombardments went about dressed in sacking or in garments confected from curtains and bed-covers. But at the many funerals, professional mourners still tore at their clothes as well as their cheeks. A problem had risen over the shortage of funeral horses, many of which had gone into the stewpot; and the most extraordinary sight of all was of two old men harnessed up with a pair of enfeebled donkeys in the shafts of a hearse. It was at a time when Naples was threatened with outbreaks of smallpox and typhoid; armed deserters from the Allied forces were attacking and looting private houses; and Moorish troops committed atrocities against men, women and children on the outskirts of the city.

The printing of occupation money, plus the devaluation of the lira from 100:£1 to 400:£1, spelled instant ruin to those dependent upon fixed salaries. An American corporal then received about ten times the pay of an Italian major, and the *Questore*, the Chief of Police of Naples, the highest paid civil servant, with a salary of 5,496 lire a month, was earning the equivalent of £14. This man was incorruptible, and I was present in his office when he fainted from hunger.

Men of lesser calibre turned to the black market, organized and presided over by Vito Genovese – and nourished by one third of all the supplies shipped through the Port of Naples for the provisioning of the Allied forces in Italy.

Children orphaned or abandoned in the anarchy of the times, the notorious *scugnizzi* (numbering perhaps 20,000), lived like little foxes in their holes in the ruins. They were outstandingly good-humoured, intelligent and beautiful, but they could only survive by pimping and petty theft. Sometimes they were driven to risk a raid on Allied food-lorries that happened to be slowed in the traffic; but this came to an end when guards were concealed in the backs of the vehicles and a number of small boys lost their fingers, hacked off by a bayonet, in the moment of grabbing a tailboard.

In families deprived of their menfolk the women frequently supported themselves and their children by prostitution. A bulletin issued by the Bureau of Psychological Warfare gave a figure for women in Naples who had become regular or occasional prostitutes of no less than 42,000. That this could have happened when there were possibly 150,000 girls of marriageable age in Naples seems incredible: there is no more convincing illustration of the extremity of their agony.

It was Naples' calvary of fire and destitution; the days of reproach through which it came at long last so astonishingly unmarred. The Neapolitans' salvation was their fortitude; their incapacity for despair. Perhaps too, there was a kind of austerity in their make-up unsuspected in Southerners – a readiness to make do with little and a lack of affinity with the acquisitiveness already beginning to dominate Western European society.

* * *

Revisiting Naples I saw it as a city that has achieved its own kind of emotional stability, is content to drift with no eye to the future, has rejected change and is unchangeable. In this way, as Scarfoglio had observed, it is Oriental rather than European. Economically it has stagnated, where the industrial North with its separate identity and ideals has pushed further and further ahead. Nearly half the Neapolitan workforce is unemployed or under-employed, but Neapolitans help each other. The income per capita is only a third of that in Milan; but, for me, Naples will always be the better place to live in.

In Naples there is a human solidarity hard to find elsewhere. If one lives there long enough one has the sensation almost of belonging to the world's most enormous family. The labour statistics may reveal situations reminiscent of Dickensian England, but there was little in the England of Charles Dickens of the laughter of Naples.

The sensation of continuity – that here in Naples one was recapturing the vanished past – was reinforced by a visit to a famous shore-side restaurant, unaltered in any way in its furnishings and atmosphere from the days in 1944 when it had been full of Allied officers and the barons of the black market. The house troubadours, facsimiles of their fathers, attended the guests as ever to strum the everlasting *Torn' a Sorrento* on their mandolins. The same algae-spotted showcase with its display of octopus and crabs was there still and so, too, was the old man hunched behind the antique cash register with its bell chiming like the Cathedral's angelus.

All the rituals had been preserved. Fish were still presented with hooks hanging from their mouths to suggest that they had been cut in that very instant from the line; and what used to be known as the 'show-fish', a majestic bass or *merou*, passed on a lordly salver from table to table to cries of admiration from diners who should have known that, whatever they ordered, it would not be this that they would eat. At the proper moment the visitors' book was produced – but here, at least, there had been changes. All the great, blustering Fascist names had been weeded out thirty-five years before, but now the pages dealing with the years 1944–45 had gone too, and with them Mark Clark, and the rest of the Allied generals. Enduring fame now belonged only to such as Axel Munthe and Sophia Loren, the local girl (surely well on her way to popular canonization) from Pozzuoli, just round the corner of the bay. Neapolitans had thrust the politicians and the soldiers out of memory.

Close to us a number of tables had been pushed together to accommodate a family later identified as a man of fifty, his wife, two teenaged children, a son in his twenties and the daughter-in-law, their three children, the host's elder brother, his widowed sister, and the grandfather, who was placed out of respect at the top of the table and to whom the show-fish was first presented for his nod of approval. In Naples there are no baby-sitters: the family takes its pleasures and suffers its tribulations as a unit, and the aged are excluded from none of its experiences.

With the exception of the eldest son, in his *moda inglese* pin-striped suit, and his stylish wife, the general impression the group gave was one of less than affluence; yet it was clear that a small fortune was being spent on this meal. By the time coffee came I found myself chatting to the head of the house. He had just been released from hospital – hence the celebration. The family went out on the town two or three times a year, he said, 'whenever an excuse can be found'. So the money went.

It was the kind of household based on a three-roomed flat – the young couple and their children would live separately – with nothing on hire-purchase, the minimum of furniture and a kitchen of the old-fashioned kind with nothing electrical in it apart from the toaster. The accommodation and home comforts of such a family might seem spartan to English people who could afford an occasional meal in an expensive restaurant.

The father went on to say that he had been employed as a mechanic in the Alfasud factory, then laid off. He added with a twinkle and a rippling gesture of the fingers that while drawing what benefits he could, he had managed to get his hands on a list of Alfasud buyers in the area and, by servicing their cars at cut price, had been able 'to keep the soup flowing'. His daughter went to school, but took time off before Christmas to make figurines for Nativity cribs, which at that season were in great demand. If necessary his wife could always turn her hand to sewing umbrellas for sale in the London stores. Should a financial emergency arise, the eldest son, who 'worked on the boats' – he nodded in the direction of the piratical launches in the harbour – could be counted on to pitch in. '*Si arrangia*,' he said: 'We get by somehow.' It has always been the true motto of Naples.

1980

INTO RUSSIA

IN OCTOBER 1944, installed at the Intelligence Corps headquarters on the first floor of the Satriano Palace, I was as ever astonished at the magnificence of the Bay of Naples as seen through the garden statuary, when the order to leave immediately for Taranto arrived. Here I was to take charge of 3,000 Russian prisoners at that moment 'in transit'. Enigmatic as this first appeared, no further information was to be obtained, so I took the first train south and after many delays arrived in Taranto in the evening of the next day.

A major in temporary command of the Russians explained their presence. They had been captured in the north of Italy while fighting in the German army and were to be repatriated by sea. I would go with them. The major exploded with wrath. 'These men are shits,' he said. 'If any man so much as attempts to escape, you will shoot him.' I warned him that such an order could not be accepted. He suddenly appeared to calm, and there was a change in his tone. 'Do they have foxes up in Naples or wherever it is you come from?' he asked. I told him that I had no idea. 'Pity,' he said. 'They do in Rome. That may surprise you. In the woods. Get one with your pistol if you're lucky.'

The Russians had been transferred to the veteran troopship *Reina del Pacifico*, and going aboard I found them in their rumpled German uniforms filling the holds and crammed into every inch of deck space. To my surprise I was to learn that all these weary, sick and demoralized men had actually turned on their German captors and gone over to the British in the first battle in which they were involved. In recognition of this they had been promised that their German uniforms would be replaced with British ones. This had not happened and a total collapse of morale had followed along with a number of suicides. Almost all the nominally Russians in sight were Asiatics, in particular from Uzbekistan, and at this moment they had begun an almost tuneless chanting described by an interpreter, who had just arrived on the scene, as a tribal funeral dirge.

A Tadjik, who was the first of these Asiatics that I could make understand me, described his experiences when captured by the Germans advancing into Russia. He and his comrades had been herded into a camp where they were held for three days without food or water before they were made to understand that they were prisoners of war. An interpreter had explained their quandary. 'There are more of you than expected,' he told them. 'There is food for a thousand, but ten thousand of you are here, so you must draw your own conclusions.'

The pick of the prisoners were enlisted in the Asiatic division sent to northern Italy and the rest eventually eliminated by starvation or outright murder, and, since regular German army soldiers were reluctant to kill prisoners, methods were contrived by which they were killed by their own comrades.

Between 4,000 and 5,000 Asiatic Russian prisoners

died, largely of starvation, in such death camps. Now, squatting among the survivors in the fetid twilight below deck of the *Reina del Pacifico*, I listened to the survivors' descriptions of the horrors that had overwhelmed them. Death's finality, these survivors admitted, was frequently confirmed by a knock on the head, after which the corpse would be smuggled away to a quiet place to be eaten. Cannibalism, at first dismissed as no more than the most impossible rumour, became a hideous commonplace to be accepted. If a man died his edible parts were eaten. Even a prisoner unconscious through sickness was liable to be attacked. One of the men I talked to displayed the cavity in the back of his leg where half the calf had been gnawed away while he was in a coma. Eventually I was convinced that all the ex-prisoners carried on this ship had eaten human flesh. The majority admitted to this without hesitation – as if the confession provided psychological release.

Authority among these survivors was divided between two men, an Uzbek mullah of the Muslim faith, and one of the handful of Christians, Ivan Golik, a Muscovite with the rank of senior lieutenant in the Red Army, whose philosophies of life were diametrically opposed. Golik's determination was at all costs to restore the fighting spirit of these cowed victims. The mullah, by the name of Haj el Haq ('the Pilgrim of Truth'), advocated death for his followers, in this case mass suicide by drowning, to be followed by life everlasting in the Muslim paradise. It was a remedy evaded by even the most fanatical of the mullah's followers by the ship's arrival at Port Said, where the promised British uniforms awaited us.

Bound to the wheels of a military machine which once

set in motion could not be stopped, ordnance spewed forth: not only the promised uniforms but a range of such army equipment as camouflage netting, gas capes, signalling flags, and above all innumerable razors and shaving brushes, the uses of which bewildered these men with hair that grew only on their heads.

It was the three-quarters of this gear that one would have supposed to have been useless that the Asiatics seized upon and converted to the ends of art, piercing, splicing and amalgamating them to provide a variety of musical instruments, tiny, antique-looking fiddles, lutes, pipes and rebecks. Soon the bowels of the ship quivered with the wild skirl of Oriental music.

Supreme theatrical art had transformed a man who had tasted human flesh into a tender princess stripping the petals from a lily while a suitor quavered a love song.

Whatever these men had suffered in the camps, nothing had been able to take their art away.

Incredibly, at last the war came to an end. I was demobilized and decided to visit Central America. I travelled to Guatemala City, where little tribal life was to be found although primitive groups of great interest had managed to survive in the Cuchumatanes mountains occupying much of the north of the country.

Guatemala was the only one of the small countries of Central America not described as being in the USA's 'backyard'. Instead it remained stubbornly resistant to all efforts to extinguish its persistent nationalism. Guatemala had held out against all foreign pressure, defended by the poverty of its resources and the absence of oil or very significant amounts of gold. The great barrier of the Cuchumatanes mountains offered better protection than the highest of walls. It was defended also by the national character and the stubbornness of some of the toughest and most dedicated of the Central American Indians.

From Guatemala City I went on to join friends at work in the highlands of Guatemala. Here they were studying the life of the Maya Indians of that area, whose existence as they reported to me was a blend both of sophistication and extraordinary spirituality. This was perhaps most apparent in the Mayan attitude to death. Their Chilam cemeteries were in the centre of the villages and the dead were seen as remaining in contact with the community and even included in family conversations and projects. These people lived wholly on maize and beans, and when these exhausted the soil in which they grew, the family, tribe, or even nation led a nomadic existence until an area where cultivation had not taken place was discovered. It was migrations of this sort that had covered Central America with the ruins of deserted cities.

I had hoped to be able to assist my friends, the Elliots, in their studies of this fascinating race, but was prevented from doing so by the landing in Guatemala of a force of mercenaries from the United States who proceeded to occupy strategic points throughout the country before overthrowing the government, and substituting a right-wing dictatorship in its place. The newcomers had a programme for a revision of the national psychology. Indian communities such as the Chilams would all become peons in the employment of farms, be paid wages, cease to grow maize and beans, and be liable for call-up in case of war. In particular, employment laws were part of the campaign to do away with Indian culture, for the Maya would now be compelled to work in slaughterhouses and even attend church. The old, stubborn and isolated Guatemala had at last joined its neighbours in the backyard.

I settled to write a book (*The Volcanoes Above Us*) about my sad adventures in Central America, which to my immense surprise eventually became a Book Society Choice for 1954. An even greater surprise was to receive a letter from the Writers' Union of the USSR to say that they would like to reach an agreement with my publishers to issue the book. It went on to suggest that it would be useful if their representative could visit this country to discuss the possibility with me.

I wrote back to say that I would be delighted to meet the Union's representative, and a week later I took a telephone call from a London hotel to announce the arrival of Valentina Evashova in this country. It was arranged that we should meet in my agent's office in Bloomsbury and it was here that our first encounter took place later in the day. A little to my surprise the distinguished professor bore a remarkable outward resemblance to a Russian peasant of the kind portrayed in one of the Soviet films to be seen in London cinemas at about that time. She was sixtyish, short and a little stout, and bundled in garments of the kind a prosperous peasant might have worn to attend a political meeting. Her expression, on the other hand, was intelligent and shrewd. She had dyed her hair dark red. She spoke rapidly in confident and faultless English. Valentina's wit was quicker than either mine or that of the agent, thus her replies to our questions were ready within split seconds of their being put.

Valentina was critical by nature and ready with instant judgements on all the problems encountered in such meetings. Her eyes ranged dubiously over the office in which she had been received. It was small and bright, but essentially modest in its furnishings and equipment. Later she made some passing comment on this and in a way it was a forewarning or reference to the grandeur of similar establishments in the Soviet Union.

Valentina had been authorized by the Soviet Writers' Union to inform me that they would print six million copies of *The Volcanoes Above Us* in paperback form. After some minutes passed without mention of any reward likely to be offered for these rights, she brought up the subject almost in passing. Russia, she said, paid no overseas royalties, but compensated foreign authors in a way most of them agreed was equally attractive. They were invited to visit the Soviet Union, not as mere tourists but as the honoured guests of the nation. The hospitality of the country was theirs to be enjoyed. They were invited to come and go where they liked, and stay as long as they liked. They could, for example, be accommodated for any length of time and without cost to them in a dacha at Sochi in the perpetual summer of the Black Sea. Guides could be given them to explore Central Asia, spend a month with a tribe in Sinkiang or hunt a unique species of boar in Outer Mongolia. As tactfully as possible I pointed out that my agent had worked very hard on the English production and marketing of this book, to which her reply was that she was sure that he too could be invited to become a guest of the Soviet Union.

On this and two subsequent occasions when Valentina visited this country on behalf of the Writers' Union we were happy to have her stay with us in Essex. It was an environment which must have seemed as exotic to her as later in my case were the Black Sea coast and the valleys of the Caucasus. As was inevitable she was out of her depth with the class system. The village policeman she glimpsed in passing while pruning his roses would be unlikely, she thought, to terrify local evildoers. She was astonished by the behaviour of a son of the local big house who had never quite recovered from his public school, but our gardener impressed her by the pleasing gravity of his expression as he demolished the weeds. 'Is he an intellectual?' she asked.

My publisher had thought fit to organize a party for Valentina, choosing the Ivy restaurant for the venue. Included were a Collins director, his film-star wife, and the uncontrollable dog from which she declined to be separated. This could not possibly have been other than a memorable experience for a woman acclimatized to the Muscovite equivalent of what the Ivy had to offer. Everyone who had done rather well in everything came here, and their gay chatter and laughter bubbled all around us. Did they laugh in Moscow? Undoubtedly, but it would not have been like this. I suspected that this gaiety was a convention, and to some extent even a practised art. I could not imagine what I had seen of the Russians fabricating mirth. Valentina had had no practice in subterfuge of this kind. As a Russian she had never been introduced to the mechanism of social pretence. Thus at our small party she was inevitably the odd one out who could not laugh things off and thus reach an easy compromise with unpalatable truth.

My forthcoming visit to the Soviet Union was soon discussed. 'Leningrad,' she said, 'is not completely recovered from the war. You should make a start with

Moscow, which offers everything of our country and life-style that the foreigner will wish to see. Be careful in crossing the street on dark nights. We have introduced new laws for car-driving, which is still to be improved. Ask the hotel porter to provide you with a torch whenever you leave the hotel after dark. It is not advisable to drive a car yourself, but if you wish to do so no charge is made for a qualified instructor to accompany you. You will be asked to avoid driving down steep hills or in the medieval district of the city where the roads are narrow. These are indicated by signs.'

Discussion of where best to go next came up and Valentina rattled off a list of historic cities and their principal attractions. 'Time is short,' she said, 'so perhaps we shall be obliged to select a very special few. Had you anything in mind?'

'Would Central Asia perhaps come into this?' I asked, a little doubtfully, and I charted the lines of disappointment in her face.

'Everything depends upon you,' she said. 'It is your choice. Central Asia is very large, but four-fifths of it is desert. Were there any towns you had in mind?'

'I thought perhaps Bukhara, or Samarkand.'

'No one may visit Bukhara at this time,' Valentina said. 'There has been an outbreak of plague. Samarkand is open to travellers. It is a capital of the tribal people, which you might not find interesting. All the same, you only have to say the word and it can be arranged.'

'You remember I told you about the tribals I took back to the Soviet Union. Most of them were Uzbeks.'

'And was there anything special about them?'

'Yes, they were natural artists. It's hard to explain. But they were in some way different. Not like us. Very few of the other tribals came through. I think the Uzbeks may have been saved by their art.'

'I'll give the Union a ring,' Valentina said, 'and if there's no plague in Uzbekistan you shall certainly go. You may need an adventurous guide who won't be too scared even if you do run into the plague. I suggest Natasha, whose background has toughened her in a way you may need. She was in Leningrad as a child at the time of the siege. The government ordered Russian civilians to stay in the city, even if they were starving. Natasha was only fourteen but her mother dressed her up as a young soldier and got her out. She speaks your language as well as you do, and she's beautiful if a little cold. When would you like to go?'

'As soon as I can,' I told her, and a week later I boarded the plane for Moscow at Heathrow. If at any time the mere boarding of a plane could be an experience, this was one. The enormous flying machine awaiting us must have been designed to represent the power of the nation that had built it. It spread its great wings over an area emptied by its lesser competitors. I climbed the twenty-two steps and trudged silently over a splendidly carpeted floor, following the stewardess. She lifted the voile curtain of the compartment I was to enter. One of its two seats was already occupied by an exceptionally well-dressed man, who rose to bow, shake hands and introduce himself. This was Dr Bryansky, a lecturer in English History at the University of Kazan.

A soft thunder of the engine extinguished the music of Borodin and the great machine moved forward, shaken suddenly as if by a mechanical palsy as it took off. A few moments passed, the red cabin light went out and the music started again, Borodin replaced by a march. What was to follow prepared me for the Russian scene that awaited me more than anything else could have done.

The passengers were on their feet, and were now moving out into the aisle. Dr Bryansky seemed about to join them. 'Shall we walk together?' he asked, and I replied, 'With pleasure.'

The aisle was now filled with two ranks of strolling passengers, and these we joined. 'What would you like to talk about?' Bryansky asked. 'Some special subject, perhaps?'

'Well, perhaps not at this moment, Doctor,' I said. 'My trouble is that I'm a writer, and I'm going to be called upon in the near future to produce a coherent description of my experiences, starting more or less now.'

'I sympathize,' Bryansky said. 'I imagine you'll be making a start with Moscow. Have you ever been there before?'

'No,' I said. 'This is my first visit to the Soviet Union.'

'You picked the worst possible time. Moscow is for spring and autumn. We shall be lucky if the plane is permitted to land if there happens to be a fog.' Bryansky's pessimistic gesture was one with which I was to become familiar, but at that moment the red light showed once more and the passengers broke up their social promenade, bowed to each other and made for their seats.

It was after dark when we landed, and spaced ranks of persons, one behind the other, awaited arrivals at the airport. Valentina, holding carnations, stood in the precise centre of the front line. I suspected that the Zil limousine seen at the kerb through the airport doors would be for us, and it was.

A room had been reserved for me at the Sovietskaya, and as we drove yard by yard through a swirling mist Valentina told me about the hotel. According to Valentina it was a quiet place, favoured by visitors concerned with the arts and sciences. It was a hotel, she said, that put itself out to make guests feel at home, and in accordance with this, dinner would feature a typical English menu in my honour. This proved indeed to be the case, our first course being Brown Windsor soup, followed by roast beef. While we tackled this, the orchestra entertained us with pieces most favoured by the British.

Valentina had a surprise for me. Only four weeks had elapsed since the signing of the contract for the book, but on this very day the first copies of the Russian version had appeared on the bookstalls. At the time there were no bookshops in the country and these horse-drawn stalls, parked at various licensed positions throughout the streets, occupied a unique position in the Soviet Union, having to some extent succeeded in remaining private enterprises.

The most energetic and successful of the bookstalls, Valentina said, were in the heart of the city, just as close as businesses could be to Red Square. This particular day was a national holiday and even our Zil limousine was only permitted to cover a short distance of Tverskaye Street – often described as the Oxford Street of Moscow. With the Kremlin in sight we continued on foot, then turned into the narrow and somewhat gloomy side-alley where the leading booksellers were in business.

Here in the dim light and gathering fog we were confronted by what appeared to be a large version of an English market-stall, from the middle of which rose a pyramid displaying stacked ranks of my books. Today, Valentina proudly informed me, was not only *The Volcanoes'* publication day, but the copies on sale here were the first delivery fresh from the press. *First Day* had been stamped on their covers, and this, Valentina hoped, added a stimulus to sales.

I was now exposed to the extraordinary sight of a queue that had formed to buy my book. Buyers were eager, the stall's owner having announced that supplies were only likely to last for a matter of days. The high sales Valentina had anticipated had made it possible to drop the book's cost to the equivalent of about three shillings. Valentina claimed that Soviet citizens were the world's most eager and voracious readers. Such prices undoubtedly helped.

Suddenly, the portrait of *The Volcanoes'* author was produced for inspection. It was a face of a visionary and a leader of men. A boldly painted eye stared confidently back at me. There was a challenge here, a firmness of purpose and courage. I looked up at Valentina, who shook her head, and we both laughed.

Valentina tackled the bookseller. 'Comrade, we both like the portrait, but it's incorrect.' He pushed his way through the buyers to talk to us, for a moment distracted by the bell chiming repeatedly on the old-style cash register in the rear. 'They never sent the real picture as promised,' he said, 'so we had make do with the best we could find. The story is that this gentleman in the picture is in French films, but who's to know the difference?' Valentina asked how many books he had sold, but he couldn't tell us, though it was 'certainly quite a number'. I examined a copy left on the counter. The cover glistened with yellowish varnish painted over a picture of a volcano erupting. In the lower right-hand corner a terror-stricken witness to the scene opened his mouth in a scream. The bookseller smiled admiringly. 'You must admit it stands out,' he said, and I had to agree with him.

I spent four days in Moscow, with Valentina always at my side. As she had promised, Valentina had persuaded Natasha to act as my guide on my tour of the country, and on our last evening together, Valentina told me a little more about my future companion. Natasha, she said, was the daughter of one of the nation's leading film stars, but she had become a figure of some importance in her own right. She spoke all the main European languages with complete fluency, and was therefore in much demand as a guide in the service of foreign visitors. My guide's arrival at the hotel next morning, however, did little to improve the Muscovite's reputation for dangerous driving. The road passing the forecourt of the hotel – a prolongation in fact of the Orel Highway – must have been one of the widest in Europe, and, like the rest of the city's streets, it was largely deserted. Knowing the Russian obsession with punctuality I was waiting with my bags by the kerb when Natasha drew up. Seconds later, with the highway still apparently empty, a taxi crashed into the back of her car. Within minutes the police were on the spot, followed almost immediately by a doctor in a sports car of local production. Natasha had been flung forward, doubled up, by the force of the crash and the doctor suspected damage to the vertebrae of her neck. At that, the doctor drove her off to the nearest hospital for an X-ray. They returned within the hour with Natasha full of smiles and the news that all was well.

As it had been announced that our plane would be delayed, we still had some time to spare. We settled in the hotel's lounge to discuss plans. Natasha was a lively, fair-haired girl, possibly in her early thirties, who spoke English – as did most Muscovites I had so far met – both idiomatically and fluently. She was clearly excited by the prospect of a journey of exceptional interest, but she was lukewarm, as most Russians appeared to be, on the subject of Central Asia. 'There is so much to be seen in the Soviet Union, and so little in the Asian steppe.' Valentina had been insistent that Sochi should be included in the itinerary. Natasha, however, was opposed to this. She shook her head, lips tightly compressed. 'I believe you will see what I mean when you get there.'

'I agree that Sochi is very beautiful,' she explained, 'and it is historically interesting due to the local opposition to the Tsarist regime, and its liberal traditions. But the place is now full of foreigners, many of whom have been persecuted in their own countries and have been invited by our government to settle there. The government houses and feeds them in exchange. This lazy life has changed their characters. It is hard to live simply when you no longer have to fight for democracy or freedom. These men behave like primitive Indians. They paint their faces and stick feathers in their hair. They expose themselves to women and sleep in the street. We can stay in this place if you wish, but I am against it. I think we should please Valentina by stopping there a day or two, and then we should go away.'

We left the hotel and caught the plane. Like all those who visit the Black Sea, we were unable to find any justification for its name. Coming in to Sochi at sunset we had circled over a vast spread of lemon-coloured water fleeced with hardly moving breakers. On landing, wonderful frigate birds tumbled out of a sky deepening to night to inspect us, and at the edge of the runway we glimpsed children oblivious to our presence, still playing with immense crabs on the beach.

An Intourist representative wearing a circus comedian's pink bowler hat was there to meet us and accompany us to our dacha. The dacha had been reserved for us for some weeks, he said, but he had to apologize for its condition. Turning on the kitchen light he was quick with a sponge to wipe out the obscene drawing on the wall. Through the window I could see the sea, now ashen in the evening light, and beyond the furthest waves a glowing ripple of the far-off Caucasian peaks.

The small incident of the drawing on the wall provided a glimmer of insight into an unexpected aspect of Natasha's complex personality. As I examined once more what was left of the damaged wall-drawing, I said, 'Pity. A good, strong picture. Quite a primitive work of art. Wonder if a fisherman did this?'

'No,' she replied, contempt twisting at the muscles of her mouth, revealing in her judgement a puritanism that came as an immense surprise.

Shortly after dawn the next morning the local council's chairman arrived to pay us a courtesy visit. The chairman – whose name, we soon discovered, was Budenin – had brought with him a posy of water-lily blooms and a basket of oven-fresh black bread as welcoming gifts. He was quick to apologize for the early hour. 'I started life as a fisherman,' he said. 'We Sochi fishermen work a fourteen-hour day, and that means an early start.' He straightened himself for his formal speech, delivered, as I had come to expect in this country, in fluent English. 'I have been asked by the members of our council to express our pleasure and satisfaction at your visit to our town,' he said, and I assured him how delighted we were to be able to visit the principal town of the Black Sea. 'Are there as many foreign visitors this year?' I asked.

Quite as many, Budenin assured us. 'Many foreign people are visiting our town at this time. You must understand that some are friends of the government. Not all these we are liking so much. Why is their behaviour so strange? My friends have all been fishermen since childhood, and we each know how the other can be expected to behave. Whatever the situation that arises, we know how our friends will confront it – how they react in pleasure, in anger or in sorrow. The foreign friends of the government who now occupy so many of the houses in this town we cannot understand, for there is no way of foretelling how they will react to any situation.'

Next day, the chairman invited us to lunch in the ancient building which the council had commandeered. He perched us on stools, as was the custom in Sochi, round a low table. 'When friends honour us with a visit,' he said, 'the main thing here is to keep fish off the menu. This means that sometimes we're down to horse. Today we're in luck. This is a kind of edible squirrel from the mountains. We like it, and we hope you will, too.'

The council building had been chosen for the commanding views it afforded over the town, and in front of us we could see the fishing boats in port, some with old-fashioned blood-coloured sails and odd cartoon figures painted on their sterns. Immediately beneath us, ancient buildings shelved steeply down to the sea. Inhabitants of this upper part of the town, the chairman informed us, were noted for their eccentric behaviour, blamed ridiculously on the thinness of the air. A citizen walking in the street below stopped to blow a whistle, at which Budenin left the table to open the window and listen to the man's news. Coming back, he assured us that there was nothing we really needed to hear, except that, as expected, the seasonal alteration in fishing times appeared to be giving trouble again.

The chairman then took his seat again and ladled food on to the plates. 'There was one bad incident last night,' he explained. 'You see, all our people are fishermen. I'm one myself. A servant of the government, if you like, but a fisherman at heart. There's a season when we fish by daylight, and another when we put out floating lights and fish at night. When the night-fishing goes on our wives sleep alone in their beds. We respect them and they respect us. That's how it should be. But now there have been certain incidents involving the foreigners – we've been obliged to appeal to the police at Sukhumi to come to our aid.'

Back in Moscow I had perhaps incautiously mentioned to Valentina my interest in wildlife and this, passed on by the Writers' Union to their representative in Sochi, had produced the offer of a small expedition on my behalf. Specialists in local fauna and flora had been alerted and I was assured that the Abkhazskaya mountain range, some forty miles to the south, was exceptionally rich in rarities of all kinds. Much of this region was virtually unknown territory, having been made accessible to four-wheeled vehicles only a few years before.

Two days after our lunch with the chairman, three specialists in animal and vegetable life arrived in a suitable vehicle. After Natasha had excused herself, we set out on a brief reconnaisance of the area most likely, as they believed, to produce results.

It turned out that two of my companions were university professors. However, the third, Colonel Vyacheslav Soldanov, was an acting army officer, and I could not repress a suspicion that he would be attracted to any adventure offered him, however small. It was a suspicion that increased when the colonel suggested our trip might offer an opportunity for exploration of a minor kind. One of the latest army four-wheel-drives had been put at our disposal, he said, and this could be used on the roughest of tracks, previously unpassable to any motorized vehicles. Soldanov claimed that with this form of transport we could reach parts of the Abkhazskaya mountain range that had never previously attracted botanical interest. I was amazed at this point to discover that my escorts had brought with them a brown paper bag containing a scimitar. This, they said, would be used to uproot interesting specimens – garden spades being practically unknown in this area of the Soviet Union.

The route suggested by the colonel was automatically accepted by the two scientists. Just as we were about to leave, however, one of the professors recalled an extraordinary event which had occurred very near the region we were to visit. A group of illicit adventurers in search of valuable minerals had suffered a catastrophe. They had been attacked by swarms of bees of an unknown kind, causing the deaths of several members of the group, and the panic-stricken flight of the survivors.

After a study of his maps the colonel assured us that we had nothing to fear from killer bees. We therefore made a start, and in the early afternoon we reached the closest of the foothills.

We found ourselves among a deserted landscape of strange shapes and exhausted colours. Walking up through the hills we came across an opening among the trees, where some freak effect, perhaps of the weather, had cleared a black little semicircle. Around us pigeons clustered like white decorations in the top branches of the pines. The Colonel was surprised – and perhaps a little disappointed – that a previous visitor had left a notice, now hardly legible, nailed to a tree trunk, advising visitors as to what could be seen. In front of us, it said, was a 'Cave of a Thousand Owls', and we watched in silence as the birds flapped in and out of sight through the black cataract of the cavern's eye. In another, smaller cave we found evidence of a now vanished human population, for it was full of skeletons packed carefully into niches by those who had interred them, with polished stones plugged carefully into the sockets of the eyes. The whole of this area was scented with the peppery odour of the pines, and there was a mysterious pinkish tint to the light, as if at the instant of sunset, caused by countless millions of tiny, winged insects that were drawn up into the stratosphere.

In these surroundings the colonel revealed himself in a new light. He believed that human mistakes over the course of the ages had caused countless damage to evolution, and despite his honours degree and senior army rank he was prepared to defend his views against all-comers. Evolution, he insisted, seemed to have fallen into a mysterious torpor – either it had come to a complete standstill or accelerated in an eccentric and incomprehensible fashion.

This, said Soldanov, was why he visited these mountains whenever an opportunity arose. It was here, according to his researches, that early man had begun interfering with the natural world. He had cut down the trees, and killed all the animals considered dangerous – the bears, the mountain lions and the poisonous snakes – but the invincible malarial mosquito and the high mountain caves full of deadly bees would always remain. These, he said, would put evolution back on course in the end. In the meantime Soldanov thought there was no place to equal Abkhazskaya for a view of what had gone wrong with the world.

Back in Sochi two days later, the Soviet Union's erstwhile foreign community was still giving trouble. The detachment of police that had been called up from Sukhumi to deal with the problem had more or less shrugged their shoulders and gone off. The chairman had ordered obscene drawings to be cleaned off the town's walls but these had immediately been replaced with others of a similar kind, although with less artistic pretension. Natasha's only news was that two respected exponents of the socialist ideal had endeavoured to further the cause of the natural presentation of the body by a naked stroll down the principal street. She was delighted to say that she had booked seats on the plane for Tashkent that would be leaving next day.

Natasha was clearly surprised to learn that we would be joined at the airport by a second guide supplied by the Writers' Union. Sergei Vilanski, an expert in Oriental history and culture, was young, handsome and above all Western in appearance and in every aspect of his manner. Although he did not admit to this I suspected him of having spent part of his childhood in our country, and there was a light-hearted cynicism about him that I found difficult to associate with a wholly Slavonic past. I took Natasha to be an orthodox communist, although such was the breadth and depth of her knowledge that nothing of this showed through. Vilanski seemed above all to be a man of the world, for whom politics were a game in which one found oneself involved willy-nilly and which one played with whatever skills one possessed or could develop.

On the plane, Natasha engaged me in earnest conversation on the subject of literature, about which she held many strong opinions. My guide – described by Valentina as the most brilliant of her pupils – turned out to be fascinated by English writers, and I learned that she had familiarized herself with the whole of William Shakespeare's opus. On rare occasions a non-Slavonic sense of humour appeared to peep out, as when she mentioned her extensive knowledge of English limericks, from which she was apparently able to extract inoffensive titbits for presentation on suitably academic occasions.

The immensely long journey to Tashkent took its effect. Vilanski's cynicism on the subject of the Socialist Motherland had been coldly received by Natasha, but, perhaps driven by boredom, he now began to lay siege to her as an available young woman. There was no place in Central Asia like Tashkent to have a good time, he insisted. The Pasha was an old friend who put him up in his palace whenever he visited. It was an Arabian Nights situation – why should she stay at a run-down hotel when he was sure he could fix it for her to have a good time in pleasant surroundings? Naturally he'd make sure that I, too, was well looked after.

'Comrade, why don't you change the subject?' Natasha said. 'Surely you can see I'm not interested.'

At Tashkent, a message left at the hotel broke the alarming news that a meeting had been arranged with the chairman of Samarkand's council for six o'clock next morning. It would take two hours to travel there by car, said the man at the desk, and one had in consequence been booked. 'Could there be some mistake?' I asked, and Natasha assured me there could not. Samarkand, she said, had established a national reputation for its prompt and efficient handling of its affairs. The city's chairman had trained himself to dispense with sleep two days a week, she had heard. Before entering politics, she added, he had been a well-known long-distance runner.

At four next morning we were ready in front of the hotel for the car. We reached our destination promptly at six o'clock, which, we soon learned, was the hour of maximum activity in Samarkand, an ancient and over-poweringly splendid town. Its centre was dominated by a cluster of mosques, each with a majestic dome roofed with tiles chosen to match the blue of the dawn sky, upon which it appeared as little more than a delicately pencilled outline. Within minutes of our arrival the town's celebrated patriarchs, white-bearded under their tremendous turbans, came on the scene in solemn procession. We watched them align themselves at exact intervals along the city's walls, where they were to remain until midday.

It was characteristic of Samarkand that our meeting with its chief citizen and the three members of his council should take place in the ancient rose gardens for which the city remains famous. The chairman, Abu Hasan, explained the function of the gathering of the bearded patriarchs we had so admired. 'They are there,' he said, 'as the embodiments of justice and truth. To become a city guardian is to fulfil any citizen's greatest ambition, and a long period may pass following a guardian's death before he is replaced. We are fortunate at this time that no places have been left empty.'

The rose gardens among which we had been received began some hundred yards from the city's centre and its assembly of magnificent mosques. It was an area that was flat and utilitarian, and planting and pruning were clearly in progress, while young apprentices were busily sweeping cuttings away. Abu Hasan was insistent that it was from precisely this spot that the garden rose had spread in its millions to all the civilized places of the world. Here 5,000 years ago the first rose as we know it had been grown to be worshipped as a spirit from heaven. Abu Hasan told us he had started his adult life as a fairly successful rose-grower, and had even exported his most valuable hybrids to European countries. These days pressure of his work for the community had limited his creative activities to three new roses a year, all of which were expected to take prizes in the annual show. One of these plants had produced a small flower that was not quite blue, and although she praised it with apparent enthusiasm in his presence, Natasha subsequently admitted that she found it bizarre.

Outside the city, the rose, having escaped captivity and blended with nature, came into its own. Abu Hasan took us up into the hills overlooking the town, where we were confronted by a remarkable scene of rambling roses spreading throughout the pines. The chairman amazed us by quoting *The Rubaiyat of Omar Khayyam* not only in the archaic Persian, but in Fitzgerald's English translation. A short walk brought us to the place where the poet had first given words to his inspiration. It was from this spot, we were told, that Samarkand's roses had begun their long journey into the hills, travelling at a rate of six inches a year. Now a brilliant floral vanguard had reached a mountain top streaked with vermilion eleven miles away.

Our excursion to see the mountain roses was only one of the attractions Samarkand arranged for its visitors. I was granted the exceptional honour of a tour of the splendid tomb of Tamerlane, although I was surprised that Natasha did not accompany me – possibly, as a woman, she was excluded from the experience. Although this was not specifically stated, it seemed likely in any case that only one visitor at a time was permitted to enter the building, for the official accompanying me remained at the entrance of the dimly lit tomb. The simple magnificence of this small, mosque-like building can hardly be equalled in the world. A flight of steps covered with onyx tiles takes one down to the basement, where, in the dead centre of the room, Tamerlane lies in his sarcophagus of jade. The legend is that when a ruler makes his pilgrimage here, the spirit of the great king may whisper encouragement to him from the grave. Absolute silence is the rule. I had removed my shoes at the entrance and as an added precaution had placed my hand over my mouth. On leaving the tomb the attendant bowed and thanked me for my ready acquiescence.

My request to see Bukhara, considered by some to be the most interesting of the ancient cities of Central Asia, was turned down as Valentina had warned me. The excuse given – that the city was still affected by the plague and was thus permitting no visitors – was readily accepted by Natasha. Vilanski, however, claimed that the authorities had closed off the city as a result of the ethnic tensions therein. In Bukhara, he said, the basically Muslim population was resisting a drive from Moscow to Westernize its Central Asian provinces. Vilanski told us that the Russian authorities were so determined to modernize these forgotten territories that they were persuading, or even forcing, Asiatics to change from Oriental to Western styles of dress. A great consignment of factory-produced (three sizes only supplied) Western-style garments had just arrived in Samarkand, he reported. He had been particularly amused by the spectacle of Asiatics, who usually wore slippers that could be kicked off in a matter of seconds when the time came to pray, wearing boots designed above all to resist the Russian snows.

The time allocated to the splendours of Samarkand was drawing to its end, and Abu Hasan informed us of his wish to throw us a farewell party in characteristic Oriental style. It was an occasion I welcomed with the greatest enthusiasm, for the chairman emphasized that his council was enthusiastically behind him in the project, designed to show their friends from the West what the East had to offer them. Unfortunately, it was an honour over which their guests were divided, for

Natasha was an out-and-out Muscovite and had made it clear to me that she had come to Central Asia only out of loyalty to Valentina. She believed that our time together would have been better spent in the cities of European Russia, which no longer – as she put it – lived in the past. Vilanski, a romantic in these matters, took the opposite point of view. For him, the Far East was steeped in colour, legend and romance, and it had been one of the high spots of his career to have been included in our excursion. He had even taken a crash course in Arabic before joining us.

Natasha proposed to repay some of our hosts' hospitality by organizing a movie show of an educational character, the films for which she had brought with her from Moscow. These specialized in sporting occasions in the capital, together with footage of young students training to become useful and well-rewarded citizens in the many excellent professions open to them in later life. Natasha's earnest proposals for the improvement of culture and opportunities in Central Asia met with outbursts of scornful laughter from Vilanski. Clearly, whatever hopes I had suspected him of harbouring for Natasha were now at an end.

Abu Hasan's party was to begin, as celebrations do in Soviet Central Asia, at roughly the moment of dawn. It was the custom in Samarkand to set off ancient bombs, shells and other explosive devices collected from old battlefields on festive occasions, and the first victims of such jollifications often expired with the first light. No instructions in the art of enjoying oneself are called for in Central Asia – it is a capacity in the blood. Above all, the celebrants are in search of sheer noise and will go to extremes to procure it. In one town some fifty miles from Tashkent two railway locomotives had been involved in a planned crash, although it was reported that casualties had been skilfully avoided.

The day of the party coincided with the feast day of a minor saint, and we woke to the ringing of holiday bells promising citizens a day of less serious occupation, although with greater rewards. A bleached sky was full of mewing sea birds, and tufts of cloud among the minarets, and as we walked over to the chairman's party we saw little girls, roused unkindly from sleep, being manacled to the lambs they were to guard during the festivities, and important old men, turbans scrupulously tied, moving like chess pieces through the morning mist towards the nearest place of worship.

There is little in the way of preliminaries to a party in Uzbekistan. Sudden action is there as if by electrical contact, and participants rise from their beds, throw on whatever clothes they can find and immediately spring to life. We moved through a throng of revellers into the town's principal square, where we were soon joined by an Uzbek tribe, bringing their special vision to the sightlessness of urban existence. Unlike the townspeople, the souls of this mysterious tribe had been preserved by a kind of holy ignorance. All of them, even the queen who led them through their deserts, preserved their illiteracy, careless that they appeared to outsiders to be lacking in intelligence. Everything they possessed, whether bought, bartered or stolen, had taken on a sacred meaning. Their wizards had painted mystic signs on their bodies and had draped themselves with soles torn from a consignment of Muscovite shoes, now promoted to fetishes.

'So you've run into them before,' someone said, and I told them about the prison ship. 'Their art saved them,' I explained. 'It wasn't food that they craved. It was bits of coloured cloth to feed the imagination.'

'They talk to their horses like children and their horses talk back,' the man said. 'Or so they tell you.'

In proof of the approaching victory of the West, time had set up its court in Samarkand. Here in the square, a large clock, imported from Moscow along with the new boots, had been fixed to the façade of an ancient fort. Soon it beat out the hour of midday – although this remained six o'clock by old-fashioned Muslim custom.

The chairman produced dancers for our entertainment and musicians accompanied them on archaic instruments. I was joined by Natasha, who, though she remained cool in her attitude to all such Oriental display, had been forced as a matter of courtesy to put in an appearance. Vilanski pushed his way over, and placing at risk any final hopes of Natasha's favour, he joined in the general acclamation of the performance. 'It is certainly interesting,' Natasha decided, 'but to be perfectly frank it doesn't appeal to me. After all, we're Westerners, and our tastes were formed in a different environment.'

The star of the occasion was a tall, muscular-looking woman who we learned was the Horse Princess, Princess Faraha, unofficial head of the Uzbek people. The chairman brought her over to us so that we might see her dance at close hand. Her arms were laden with bangles to the elbow, and she wore a species of veil currently in fashion, which reached only to the tip of her nose. The accompanists beat their tambourines and she went into a short but highly Oriental dance routine in which the muscles of her stomach were put to remarkable use. It was a dance I greatly enjoyed, but inevitably it called forth Natasha's wrath. Although it did not seem impossible that Princess Faraha understood English, Natasha turned to me and remarked loudly and insultingly on the spuriousness of the proceedings. 'The Princess's people are from the Sholdava Steppe,' Natasha said. 'They still live on the wild sheep they hunt on horseback.'

I asked if there was any possible chance of seeing them in action. The Princess seemed about to reply when Natasha cut in. 'I'm sure that something could be arranged for you through the Ministry,' she said, 'but I warn you that these people are still quite primitive, and any photographs you might be able to obtain are not likely to be suitable for public exhibition.'

As soon as the entertainment was at an end, the Princess knelt to receive her traditional reward. Only a few years before this would have been a gold coin first pressed against her forehead then handed over with due ceremony, but now the chairman simply passed her a fifty-rouble note.

Thus gold had turned to paper, and what would once have been an audience dressed in the tribal splendour described by travellers of the past had become a crowd clad in mass-produced garments from Russian factories. How sad it seemed that these people who had designed and cultivated the first rose gardens of the world and built these overpowering mosques should now be obliged to turn their backs on colour and clothe themselves in the uniforms of a utilitarian world.

At the party I had met a native of Tashkent who had emigrated to the States and lived there for two years before his return. Since the building of Tashkent's airport he had been employed by the region's developing tourism industry, and his special responsibility was the opening up to the public of the Sholdava steppe – one of the great unexplored places of the world. I spoke to him at length about the project, and he was ready with a series of convincing replies.

'You heard of the snowmobile?' he asked. 'We're all set up to make snowmobiles for sand.'

'What is there to see?' I asked.

'Pygmy sheeps,' he said. 'Same size as not big dog. You ever see pink rats? You gonna see them there. One mountain lion used to be around but now old. Maybe dead. Anyway no trouble.' The sandmobile, he said, would follow the routes used by the horsemen of old. The great problem, of course, was that the steppe was in a perpetual state of change.

'One day big hill, next day wind comes and is small hill. No tribes, only families. One husband, two wives. If a woman finds man to feed her she will marry that man. When no more food, she will go away.'

'That is sensible,' I said.

'Not only one Sholdava,' he went on, 'are many steppe. The rulers live in highest places and food is brought to them. The Horse Princess comes also to all these places. If a ruler feeds her she may marry him for a short time. Then she will go.'

'And someone else will feed her?'

'That is why she is princess.'

'If I provide the food would she marry me?'

'Maybe you are not too much for her in some way, but I think that she will.'

My new friend promised to take me to see the steppe, and we set off together on a day-trip early the next morning. In the late afternoon we reached a small, ruined town, beyond which the steppe's frontier of pale greenish gold shone in the distance, a glistening, emptied world forming a small corner of a forgotten universe.

I soon saw why my friend had found it almost impossible to write a tourist guide to the great steppe, for even as we studied the horizon through our binoculars the view changed.

'You go look for mountain there yesterday, and that mountain is not there today,' my friend repeated. 'A week passes and nothing the same. If wind is OK comes smell of peaches, but then it changes, and you cover nose from smell of death.'

After the success of our excursion, it was decided that we should make a longer exploration of the steppe, but the next day my friend failed to appear. In his stead his representative arrived at the wheel of an old Ford V8 fitted with extra large wheels and oversized tyres. He was a pure Uzbek, small, dark and eager to please. Unfortunately, he was the possessor of the difficult name of Vloc, which sometimes produced a titter when I attempted its pronunciation. The sandmobile was not ready, he said, assuring me in a mixture of Russian and English that this was all to the good. 'In Ford we get there,' he explained, 'in sandmobile, maybe.' A brusque change in the weather accompanied the appearance of this unexpected form of transport. It had rained during the night for the first time in two months, and the sky was clotted with plum-coloured clouds.

A shapeless human form under the blanket covering the back seat caused a few moments of confusion. To my surprise, after the removal of the covers this shape became recognizable as the Horse Princess, and I now remembered some mention at the time of the chairman's party of her forthcoming visit 'to my steppe'. The change in her appearance was remarkable. She was wrapped in the unflattering garments of a working woman. Gone were the bangles and necklaces, and the shadowed eyelids were no more. But, above all, I was astonished to see that no trace of the vulgar paint-assisted fairground good looks of two days before remained. They had been replaced by an air of unmistakable intelligence. I felt a certain relief that Natasha had declined to accompany me.

We were headed, I was told, for the village where the Princess had been born. 'They call it a village,' Vloc said, 'but there are only four or five huts, with more horses than humans living in them.' While we were discussing our prospects a rent appeared in the sky's grey covering, rain poured down and almost instantly smoke began to rise from the sand. It would dry, Vloc said, in a matter of hours – especially close to the hills where the drainage was good. As we had come to a halt, he broke out the food he had brought in case of emergencies – in that part of the world they fell back on edible worms in times of shortage – and he showed me the offerings he proposed to place in front of the horse shrines should we receive a hospitable welcome at our destination.

The rain soon stopped and we reached the village well before dark. A tiny man came out of a hut. Black hair fell to his shoulders and he was without front teeth. 'Bow to the shrine,' he said, and the Princess took us behind the hut to a mound under which the horses were buried, and I made my obeisance.

'They passed a law making us Christians,' Vloc

explained, 'but when one of us dies a note goes into his grave saying that he refuses to be resurrected. If there's no way out of it we ask to be resurrected as horses.'

Next day he offered me a tiny pony to accompany him on a visit to areas which were out of reach by car. 'They pray to horses there,' he added as an inducement, 'and hang flowers round their necks.' My stallion in miniature threw me as soon as I mounted it. 'It must be the smell he can't stand,' Vloc said. 'We could rub you down with salt. That might do the trick.'

The salt was then applied, but with little success, for mounting under Vloc's supervision the most docile of his ponies, I held on for only a few yards before being thrown over its head. Thereafter we trudged through squelching sand to a neighbouring village where garlanded horses were indeed in view. This may have been the steppe's first attempt at transforming an authentic folk ceremony into a tourist attraction. On our arrival, young Uzbeks had been sent scurrying off into the dunes for flowers; a little while later a few returned bearing long trailers of what might have been a coarse and bedraggled version of convolvulus. While Vloc mumbled what he said was a prayer, the villagers hung the resulting garland round a horse's neck, after which it was removed and given to the animal to eat.

Vloc had spent much of his childhood on the steppe, but he admitted that he no longer wished to stay here more than a few days – nowadays, he claimed, he was dependent on Russian food, not to be had in these backward places. When deprived of Russian bread in particular, he said, he began to feel weak after three days. The villagers had recently announced a godsend, in the form of a swarm of large edible flies, and the pessimism with which he received this erstwhile good news only served to emphasize the gap between his present state and his past.

Vloc clearly took (or pretended to take) the edible flies incident as an omen that we should depart, but, I asked, what was to be done about the Horse Princess? Was she staying on the steppe, or did she intend to return with us? Vloc said that he did not know her intentions, or whether arrangements should be made on her behalf. When he finally thought of asking the Princess herself, she replied that she would stay. She had returned to her people, after an absence of many months, to count the number of her tribe, she said. She was pleased to announce that this had increased by one. But she was worried about her horses. The Uzbeks could not be relied upon to deal with numbers, she was sorry to say, and she had come above all to be sure that the number of animals was not on the decrease.

I returned to Tashkent, where Natasha was waiting for me at the hotel. As I walked through the door nothing moved in the calm of that serene Slavic countenance. 'Lucky you got in early,' she said. 'There's been a plane cancellation and we have to take off tomorrow.'

'Couldn't be better,' I said.

'How about the steppe?' she asked. 'Did you enjoy it?'

'I did. You'd have enjoyed it, too.'

'I'll phone Valentina straight away,' she said. 'She'll be delighted. So it was a success in every way?'

'It was a totally new experience,' I explained, 'and an immense surprise. Did you manage to amuse yourself in Samarkand while I was away?'

'I visited more rose gardens, then Vilanski drove me

here,' Natasha said. 'This is one of those quiet places where news soon gets round. They tell me the Horse Princess is back on the steppe.'

'She was. I saw her; in fact I travelled with her. But not for long. She was on the move.'

'Did they go in for a great deal of dancing wherever it was that you went?' Natasha asked.

'No, because it's no more than the simplest of existences. The Horse Princess dances in the towns and puts the money to good use on the steppe. There they call her the teacher.'

'And what does she teach?'

'How to care for spider bites, calm lunatics and keep out the sand.'

Natasha nodded her agreement. 'And what could be better?'

'Another thing she teaches,' I said, 'and out there on the steppe it's the most important thing of all, is resignation. I told you about the prison ship and the Uzbeks who were going to be shot? They knew it would happen, but they didn't seem depressed in the slightest. They kept up their laughter and joking all the time. It was just about the only laughter you heard on that ship.'

'It's the old Muslim thing, I suppose,' Natasha said. 'Put up with it. It is written.'

'I often wonder what happened to them. Do you imagine Valentina might be able to find out?'

'I'm sure she'll try if you ask her. Anyway, we'll see her tomorrow. She's certain to be at the airport to meet the plane.'

2001